WAYS UNTO HEAVEN
(*Masãlik-ul-Jinãn*)

By

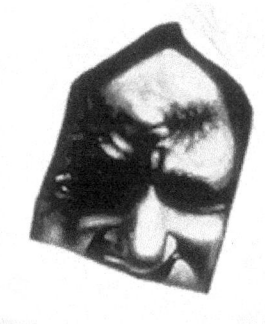

SHEIKH AHMADOU BAMBA
(1853-1927)

The African Muslim Leader of Nonviolence
And Founder of the Muridiyya
(Senegal, West Africa)

English Translation and Commentaries by

Abdoul Aziz Mbacke
Leader of the Majalis Research Project and
Head of the Institut Khadimou Rassoul (IKHRA)
www.majalis.org

ISBN 978-0-578-01549-1

"Bamba's sacred literary legacy remains for the most part untranslated into Western languages from Arabic and Wolof. The total number of works on Bamba in English are relatively few, even though, as David Robinson writes, Bamba became one of the most outstanding poets and mystical leaders of the last 100 years...Further study into the contribution Bamba made in the cultural and spiritual revival of his people will demonstrate the significance his universal message and nonviolent struggle has for attaining peace in the world today."

Michelle R. Kimball

Sheikh Muhammad Mourtada Mbacke,
son of Sheikh Ahmadou Bamba, reading the Qur-ãn

Preface

I wish to dedicate this work to the late Sheikh Muhammad Mourtada Mbacke, who never spared any efforts and any pains to spread peacefully the true word of Islam throughout the world, in spite of his old age. This translation is the right outcome of his work. Thank you *Goor Yàlla*.

I wish also to acknowledge all who contribute in whatever form to the publication of this book. May they all be eternally rewarded thereof by the Almighty Lord.

This book was written in Arabic by Sheikh Ahmadou Bamba during his thirties, before he became famous, owing to 33 years of tense relationship with the French colonial authorities. Sheikh Ahmadou Bamba is an African Muslim Sufi master, born in 1853 in Senegal (West Africa), during French colonization, just after the official abolition of slavery in the colonies. He was born into a renowned Muslim clerical family, the Mbacke, well-known for their deep-rooted attachment to learning and teaching religious knowledge. Islam had then nearly a thousand years of history in Senegal.

Showing precociously gifted inclination towards learning and imitating the noble devout Sufis he heard about, Sheikh Ahmadou Bamba started, in his early youth, to write books devoted to the fundamentals of religious knowledge any believer is compelled to know—Islamic Law (*Fiqh*), Theology (*Tawhīd*), Spiritual education (*Tarbiyya*), Sufism (*Tasawwuf*) etc. His high concern to preserve and to spread in an easier form true knowledge and the valuable Islamic principles among his people led him to put in verses many of the reference prose books of that time he found too hard-learning for most of his contemporaries. *Masālik-ul-Jinān* (Ways unto heaven) belongs to this category of books.

During the years following *Masālik*, Sheikh Ahmadou Bamba founded the first Muslim brotherhood ever been founded by a black

5

man in all Islamic history (the Muridiyya) and settled new forms of teaching he thought more suitable to his disciples and more likely to rekindle their human dignity depreciated by long years of political and intellectual domination. Many from all around the country, from all social classes, came to join the revival movement he initiated through teaching and worshipping God in accordance with the Sunnah of the Prophet (PBH) and with the rules of Sufism. Thanks to his charismatic virtues and to the spiritual lights his disciples were shining, his reputation soon expanded and crowds towards his *daaras* (schools) fast took larger proportions.

Such a trend aroused a libelous campaign against Sheikh Ahmadou Bamba, from some native colonial representatives, and provoked strong mistrust to the French colonial power who suspected him of preparing his disciples to *Jihad* (holy war). This bias was all the most unfair if we consider the nonviolent philosophy of the Sheikh as well as his concept of *Khidma* (Rendering Service to the Prophet) which excluded any violence, even against the vilest creature. Indeed the kind of spiritual and intellectual *jihad* the Sheikh was carrying on was quite different from all what was known by western people about Muslim leaders' resistance. The Sheikh wrote on this purpose: **"I am waging my Jihad through Knowledge and Fearing the Lord"**. However, regardless of such kind of concern, the colonial authorities decided to arrest and deport him to Gabon (Central Africa), in September 1895. After eight years of a very trying exile, during which the Sheikh wrote, in loneliness, an impressive number of poems all dedicated to the Lord and His Messenger (PBH), the French decided to let him go back home, in November 1902. But, in fearing his growing charisma over the masses aroused by his success, they exiled him again to Mauritania, afterwards they maintained him in house arrest in Senegal until his death in 1927. However history proved later that colonial strategies of "containment" did not succeed in holding back Sheikh Ahmadou Bamba's teachings and work from shaping deeply the thoughts and the culture of his nation and of millions of people all around the world.

Abdoul Aziz Mbacke
Touba, January 2009

Abbreviations used

d.   = date of death.

h.   = year of the Hijra (the beginning of Islamic Calendar); usual subsequent date put in brackets represents the corresponding year in Christian calendar.

p.   = page.

Qur-ãn xx. 25 = *Sũrah* 20, Verse 25 of the Holy Book.

Cf.   = compare.

PBH   = Peace and Blessings be upon Him (the Prophet).

lit.   = literally.

"The Sheikh" and "the Servant of the Prophet" refer to Sheikh Ahmadou Bamba.

Transcription of Wolof and Arabic nouns follows sometimes the usual forms better known.

Extracts from another book of the translator "JIHAD FOR PEACE"

A MESSAGE FOR HUMANKIND

Masālik-ul-Jinān is a book about Sufism, written by the African Muslim master, **Sheikh Ahmadou Bamba**, who wrote it within 1883 and 1887 (1300-1304 h.), at the beginning of his thirties. This corresponds to the period following his father's death, when he started expressing openly his profound leaning towards the pattern of the Pious Ancients. "Ways unto heaven" is an exhaustive digest of the highly valuable teachings bequeathed by the old Sufi Masters, which are expounded and explained with a rare genius by the Sheikh in this book entirely versified in Arabic.

However, we have to bear in mind that a Sufi author surpasses an ordinary scholar that is displaying his theoretical knowledge about spiritual questions. Indeed, we may feel through the notable synthetic mind of his verses that the *Servant of the Prophet* was one who was putting into rigorous practice the principles that are in this book - which was amply demonstrated later by his very existence - and one who have got preciously a keen experience of Sufism (*Cf.* The Biography of Sheikh Ahmadou Bamba - Tome IV, Appendix 1).

Masālik is mainly based on a previous prose work, written by Al-Yadālī[1], a Mauritanian master, entitled "*Khātimatu-t-Tasawwuf* " (The Seal of Sufism), which content is supplemented here by a wide range of writings of other Sufi Masters, admirably summarized by the Sheikh. However, notwithstanding the high significance of reliable and accredited sources in Islamic theology - which commonly

---

[1] *Cf.* Annex of the authors (Tome IV, at www.majalis.org/masalik). See also all references of our quotations at this same URL.

compels Muslim writers to fasten to the *taqlīd* (the opinions of the Ancients) – we must not infer therefrom slavish plagiarism or lazy eclecticism. Because such knowledge as *Tasawwuf* consists not in mere academic learning or formal quotations, but it has to be individually experienced and lived, so as to be fully understood. This explains most certainly why Sheikh Muhammad Bachir Mbacke (1895-1966), son and biographer of Sheikh Ahmadou Bamba, was keen to point out in the biography he devoted to his father [2]:

> *"Our Sheikh – may God be Satisfied with him- has revived Sufism inasmuch as he revived Sufi practice and Suluk (commitment in the spiritual path). He composed [in this purpose]* **Masãlik-ul-Jinãn** *(Ways unto Heaven), which is a versification of Al-Yadãli's* Khãtimatu-t-Tasawwuf, *and he put in that book a great number of rules and recommendations - sometimes summarized, sometimes detailed - so as to let people know that it is a versification of Al-Yadãli's book, in respect for its noble author. But there is no doubt that [Ways unto heaven] is far richer than Al-Yadali's original text. Yet, his deference prevented the Sheikh from separating distinctly his personal thoughts from that text [in which case his book would no longer be called a versification of Al-Yadali's book]...While putting a previous prose book in verse, [the Sheikh] never failed to insert into his writing what was springing out of his vast intelligence and out of his heart, that is; renouncing this vile world, loving God and preferring the Future Life.""* [3]

Through *Masãlik*, we are given a comprehensive idea of the moral and spiritual attitudes enabling man to get round material obstacles and countless worldly temptations which prevent him from getting nearer to the Lord. Thus, it constitutes *"a remedy for any such whose heart has been dulled by earthly lusts"* (verse 27) and a first-rate

---

[2] Entitled *Minanu-l-Bãqi-l-Qadim* (The Favors of the ETERNAL GOD) in which are gathered highly valuable biographical accounts relating to his father's life, some he personally witnessed.

[3] All the references of our quotations are available at this URL; www.majalis.org/masalik.

viaticum for all who aspire not to yield to the luring mermaids of modern life and to purify their hearts. This is part of the reasons why we felt the necessity to undertake the translation of its 1563 verses in English, so as to allow English-speaking people to get to know the priceless contribution of Sheikh Ahmadou Bamba in Islam, in upholding and handing down to present and future generations the very "substance" of the Eternal Message. And books like *Masālik* provide us with the essential keys to enter the kingdom of this universal and timeless Message.

MUSLIM NONVIOLENCE

Indeed this universal message of peace and worship of Sheikh Ahmadou Bamba to humankind is nowadays worthier than ever of careful thought. The world today is threatened by growing ruthless collision between Western conception of life and the Islamic approach of human freedom endorsed by a group of Muslims labeled as "extremists" or "terrorists". Recently, such a worldwide coldblooded struggle reached horrendous heights with September 11 attacks, the thousands victims of Iraq and Afghanistan wars, and never-ending armed conflicts in the Middle-East and all around the world.

Beyond real geopolitical and strategic or even strictly "religious" motivations, we contend that the deepest driving forces of this conflict are to be sought as well in the differing perspectives of the two systems, schematically taken, about *human rights and duties*, their true meanings and their limits in the universe. Such a "cultural" discrepancy is exacerbated by blatant lack of balance and of appositeness shown on either side in opposing their variances in the field of political interests. Western fanatic materialism and excesses - which led man to lose track of his own meaning and reality in the universe - is facing fierce religious activism - which went also far astray beyond the limits imposed by minimum respect for human life. Every disproportionate stance of one side produces unbalanced responses from the other side, thus providing higher levels of hatred and misunderstanding to the dreadful escalation—unfairness always calls for unfairness. So, what both sides need is more balance and more clear-sightedness. Sheikh Ahmadou Bamba's teachings and spiritual perspective of Islam offer this unhoped-for balanced model.

The Jihad of Knowledge and Worship

"And let not the hatred of others to you make you swerve to wrong and depart from justice. Be just: that is next to piety: and fear God."
(Qur-ãn v. 8)

In practicing such a Divine Order, Sheikh Ahmadou Bamba made clear the true nature of his fight in a poem written in 1903, on the point of leaving for his second exile to Mauritania:

" *[O ye my persecutors!] ye banned me on the pretence that I am waging a war* (Jihad) *against you. Indeed ye are right because I am really combating for the Countenance of the Lord.* **But I am waging my Jihad through Knowledge** (ulũm) **and Fearing the Lord** **(taqwã),** *as [an humble] subject of God and the servant of His Prophet; and the Lord who oversees everything may assuredly bear witness thereof… While others hold material weapons to be feared, my two weapons are [knowledge] and [worship]; and this is surely my way of fighting."* (Cf. his poem "O ye People of the Trinity!").

Indeed, it may be somewhat unexpected to many, in our context of tarnished perception of Islam, widely portrayed, through mass media, as intolerant and intrinsically violent, to hear a Muslim leader, who was yet victim of glaring injustice from unbelieving rulers during 33 years, defending nonviolence, forgiveness and love for humankind. The following verses, taken from some Bamba's poems, may assuredly show how Islam, if really understood and lived, can be tolerant and how it integrates *organically* all the high morals which lead man to surpass himself:

"I have forgiven all my enemies for the Countenance of the Lord who turned them away from me for ever, because I feel no resentment against them."

"O Supreme Master of the universe! O Thou that art beyond any resentment, grant Thy mercy to all the creatures, o Thou who guide those who go astray!"

"May all humankind benefit from me, o Lord!"

"Make me a source of bliss for all, black and white"

"Spare me ever damaging Thy creatures, be they living near me or afar, be they Muslims or unbelievers."

"O Lord! Lift me to the rank of Renovator of the Path of Islam, out of any hostility and war."

"O Lord! Spare me ever harming any of Thy creatures and protect me from their harm as well."

"O Lord! To whomever that is blaming me or who has offended me, forgive him and may he submit to Thee."

"Impart Thy Guidance, thanks to me, to the people of my time and to coming generations"

"The true warrior in God's path is not he who kills his enemies, but he who combats his ego (nafs) to achieve spiritual perfection"

"Indeed, the toughest Jihad consists in hindering one's mind from ever involving in aught that is not proper."

"Always cherish good feelings for all the creatures of God."

Such a peaceful and high attitude led Michelle R. Kimball, founder of the International Peace Project, to entitle "**A Muslim Peacemaker of the Twentieth Century - Shaykh Ahmadou Bamba**" her introduction to the book "Shaykh Ahmadou Bamba and Qur'anic and Sunnah Foundations of the Muridiyyah Order". She wrote:

"Amidst the heightened state of turmoil in the world today, associated with the apparent clash between Islamic and Western cultures, the life of one Muslim peacemaker warrants recognition - a Muslim saint who led a successful and completely nonviolent struggle for peace within the last century...Beyond the value of Bamba's life and teachings for specific ethnic groups, he is a reminder of the adaptability and universality of the religion to different cultures and peoples through its inner tradition...Further study into the contribution Bamba made in the cultural and spiritual revival of his people will demonstrate the significance his universal message and nonviolent struggle has for attaining peace in the world today."

In another article of "The Economist", titled *"Faith in the market"* (December 19th, 2006) and devoted to Murids' economic doctrine and industriousness, the author concluded:

"Little known as they are, the Murids might have a lot to teach the rest of the world—not only about how to respond to globalization, but how to practice religion in a peaceful way."

Indeed, hitherto very little is relatively known about the richness of Sheikh Ahmadou Bamba's philosophy and teachings in the world today, particularly regarding his method of nonviolent resistance. Bamba succeeded in combining perfectly standing up for his faith and for his moral principles with acknowledging to others the right to live peacefully, as long as they try not to constrain him violently to give up his faith. Such a philosophy warrants certainly a certain examination so as to know its doctrinal and historical grounds.

Divine Guidance vs Human Strategy and Wisdom

It is noteworthy that the kind of nonviolence advocated by Bamba is quite different, to many extents, to that claimed by Gandhi or by Martin Luther King. As some have noticed it, both Gandhi and Martin Luther King were killed through *violence*, although their being calling publicly for *nonviolence*. According to the Muslim perspective taught by Sheikh Ahmadou Bamba, this is not at all contradictory since, as

14

worthy and as wise as Gandhi and King's strategies might be, they are just human and rational *strategies* issuing from their only reasoning and beliefs. Even the deep spirituality referred to by Gandhi, although morally valuable and praiseworthy, it has no ultimate effectiveness and a *spiritual* value in the pure Islamic view. Since the principle of *Ahimsa* (the avoidance of violence) he was claiming originates from the religions of ancient India (Hinduism, Buddhism and Jainism) which are ranked among pagan and polytheistic beliefs or among mere philosophies by Islamic orthodoxy. *Ahimsa* notably emphasizes vegetarianism and bans hunting and ritual sacrifice, contrary to Islam. As for M. Luther King's nonviolence, it was primarily a useful strategy, inspired by Gandhi's struggle and philosophy. Besides, it is known that King was counseled to adopt this strategy by Bayard Rustin, an African American civil rights activist, who has studied Gandhi's teachings and who was well-known for his open homosexuality and his former ties with the Communist Party USA.

Human rational wisdom and rationality may well lead to success as it may lead to failure or to transitory setbacks which could end in future success. But, according to the Muslim beliefs and Sufi philosophy referred to by Sheikh Ahmadou Bamba, man has to submit his entire will to his Lord and to worship Him perfectly, in purifying his heart from all worldly vanities and desires aside from God, so as to attain true spiritual perfection which enables him to benefit from direct Divine guidance.

*"**Fear God** and God will **teach** ye."* (Qur-ãn ii.282)

*"O ye who believe! If ye **fear God**, He will grant you a **criterion** (to judge between right and wrong)."* (Qur-ãn ii.282)

*"This is the Book; in it is **guidance** sure, without doubt, to those who **fear God**. "* (Qur-ãn ii.1)

*"And those who strive in Our (cause),- We will certainly **guide** them to our Paths: For verily God is with those **who do right**."* (Qur-ãn xxix.69)

*"So persevere patiently: for **the End** is for those who are **righteous**."*
(Qur-ãn xi.49)

According to Sheikh Ahmadou Bamba's philosophy, God's direct teaching goes far beyond any rational strategy or human wisdom, and leads inevitably to ultimate success. In fact, that is real wisdom and clear-sightedness. Man can attain it only through Fear of God (*taqwã*), which is defined by the masters as "complying perfectly to God's Orders and avoiding all He forbids". (Fear of God is often equivalent to worship and to good deeds, in Muslim vocabulary.)

Thence, the kind of spiritual Jihad promoted by Sheikh Ahmadou Bamba is quite different from that advocated by many modern Muslim "activists" as well. Inasmuch as the Sheikh wishes that Muslims may first perfect their faith, their trust in the Lord, their commitment to knowledge and worship, their behaviors and their morals through education and clear-sighted determination (*himmah*). Otherwise, their faith would remain a void principle which could not in the least shield them from being dominated by other civilizations and from losing their spiritual strength, whatever arms they may use. The real quintessence of Islam, which gave Muslims power and success in every domains, in the past, was unfailing fidelity to the spiritual and moral principles taught by the Holy Book and by the Sunnah of the Prophet (PBH), revived and further theorized through Sufi masters' teachings. God promises His help only to the true believers who fear Him really, not to zealous formal worshippers; as He asserted *"Verily God will defend **those who believe**"* (Qur-ãn xxii.38). Such a dialectical principle of Faith-Guidance is the spiritual basis of Bamba's thinking, as implied by his writings;

*"[O Lord!] Impart me **Righteousness** and Thy **Guidance**, protect me from blame and grant me Worthiness by the Grace of the Prophet." "God, the Creator, has **guided** me [on His Path] and has led me to Him through all kinds of wonders. The Matchless Lord has freed me from anything but Him and has led me [on the Right Path]." "I render thanks to the Supreme Protector who has protected me from all my enemies."*

Because, in Bamba's view, that is Divine Guidance which has provided him protection and which has ensured his success, unlike preceding Muslim resistance fighters in Senegal who all failed to oppose to French colonizers, because they did not attain such a spiritual degree.

Although Sheikh Ahmadou Bamba did not dismiss absolutely or exclude the possibility to use material weapons, in case of self-defense or under the special circumstances provided for by Islamic law, his spiritual degree inspired him to use instead other kinds of *weapons* more suitable to his space and time—combating his own soul, purifying his heart and consecrating his entire life to raise the Divine Word and to benefit all humankind (*khidma*) so as to be guided and protected by the Creator Himself. According to this new perspective, if the Prophet (PBH) decided at a certain point to take up arms and to combat unbelievers, it was only after clear permission was given to Him by the Lord Himself, but not just through personal strategy or human aggressiveness. The word *jihad* itself conveys a wider etymologic meaning, that is "efforts" made in God's Path.

Was it not such a mystical perspective, the Sheikh could have certainly followed the same violent model chosen by many previous Sufi resistance fighters who combated French colonialists through arms. Is evidence thereof what he said after the trying and frustrating hardships the French Governor of Dakar made him undergo on the way to exile (September 1895):

> "Whenever I recall my sojourn in such a [awful prison] they put me in, and the [misbehavior] of that unfair governor, I feel like taking arms [to combat them]. But **the Prophet himself dissuades me** therefrom."

This verse is an evidence of the spiritual perspective Sheikh Ahmadou Bamba gave his nonviolent struggle, which goes beyond mere human reaction of indignation and of revolt against glaring injustice, and which takes its roots from mystical motivations. Books like *Masālik-ul-*

Jinãn (Ways unto heaven) provide us with the vital groundwork to better understand the basic principles which can lead to this kind of spiritual philosophy.

Extracts from "JIHAD FOR PEACE"
By Abdoul Aziz Mbacke

Translator's note

Indeed translating the *Masālik* was not an easy task inasmuch as the allusive style imposed by the constraints of versification made it sometimes very arduous to render accurately into perfect English the basis of the original Arabic text. Fortunately, a previous French translation of this book has already been performed in 1979 by the late Serigne Sam MBAYE (God be Satisfied with him) who did so the spadework regarding equivocal references; which contributed much to facilitate our undertaking. (May the MERCIFUL LORD reward him for his immense contribution and his providing light to many who committed themselves in the Kingly Path towards the Lord.)

However purist readers of the original Arabic text may be sometimes disconcerted by some "liberties" we happened to take with it as far as certain particularly arduous passages were concerned, or when we came across verses which, in our opinion, couldn't be fully understandable for a Western trained mind without taking particular classification standards. Here are some of such reorganization measures we decided to adopt to make our text easily readable:

☞ We have decided to publish this translation in two forms:

1. A digital complete version which include 4 parts corresponding to

❶ The preamble of *Masālik* (660 verses)

❷ The two first chapters: The Creatures (211 verses) and The Serious Vices (216 verses)

❸ The third chapter: Muslim Ethics (*Adab*) (476 verses)

❹ Two Appendixes (relating to the main points of Sheikh Ahmadou Bamba's biography and the holy city he founded (Touba)), four annexes including the biographies of the authors quoted in the *Masālik,* and the references of our quotations

You can access this complete version at this URL www.majalis.org/masalik.

2. This lightened book version which includes all the 3 first above-mentioned parts except few sections dealing with particular acts of worship or phrases of invocations liable to burden somewhat a reader not familiar to Islamic spirituality enough.

☞ We have followed the original subdivision of the book into chapters and sections even if we have added now and then other divisions liable to show better the logical linking of certain parts

☞ The verses are numbered (as in the French translation) although we happened at times to group together some adjacent verses which relate intimately to the same theme

☞ To avoid letting the usual digressions of religious poems (pleas, calling for blessings, harangues and so) distract the reader from the main point of the text, we have chosen to skip them or to write such parts in italics.
Example:
72- [I beseech my LORD] in the name of our Beloved Prophet Aḥmad, the Accredited Intercessor - *may Peace and Blessings be ensured, for aye, to him*

☞ Every time we came across neighboring verses among which one is the necessary complement of the others, we added suspension points before the completing verse.
Example:
73- *...As to his Family, his Companions and all that will follow in his footsteps, till the Day of Trials*

☞ As for obvious quotations, we put them in italics and in bold.
Example:

54- Do call to thy remembrance, thou that art scorning my work, this Prophetic maxim (*hadith*): *"My community is like a rain, [no one knoweth which part thereof is the best; the first part or the last part]"*

☞ GOD's Attributes and Fine Names are in capital letters (as a sign of awe and veneration); as for words which relate to Eminent Figures of Islam we just put their first letters in capital.

☞ We have also tried to go a bit farther than the French translation as far as footnotes are concerned. So one can find in this work many notes likely to clarify certain points or to show the pertinence of some maxims according to the Holy Book and various accredited sources. Naturally any who would find it laborious to always refer to footnotes and would content himself with the text itself (so as to lose not the thread) may well disregard these.

☞ A certain number of diagrams and annexes have been attached to the digital version, so as to give a synoptic view of some particular questions.

We are infinitely indebted to the admirable Interpretation of the Qur-ãn performed by Yusuf Alï, for its concern about construing in accessible and accurate English many Islamic concepts and notions. Thus, as one may notice it, did we not deny ourselves imitating sometimes its "religious" and classical style (whose beauty has also the virtue to contrast holy writings with secular writings) while trying however to avoid overusing ancient English forms liable to cumbersome such a style for modern readers.

Thus, we make ours, with due allowances, this preface of Yusuf Ali to the first edition of his famous English translation of the Qur-ãn in 1934:

"Gentle and discerning reader! what I wish to present to you is an English Interpretation… The English shall be, not a mere substitution of one word for another, but the best expression I can give to the fullest meaning which I can understand from the Arabic Text. The rhythm, music, and exalted tone of the original should be reflected in the English interpretation.

It may be but a faint reflection, but such beauty and power as my pen can command shall be brought to its service. I want to make English itself an Islamic language, if such a person as I can do it, and I must give you all the accessory aid which I can."

However, we do humbly admit that rendering quite rigorously the content of *Masālik* (for lack of its admirable form) is a pretence we are far from claiming to achieve. Future editions will be in charge of correcting possible mistakes and noticed misconceptions. So if there are any mistakes or misinterpretations in the text we put forward here, we do beseech our BOUNTIFUL LORD - the MOST MERCIFUL of those who show Mercy - to grant us His Pardon and not to call us into account thereof in the Hereafter, HE Who said:

"O My Servants who have transgressed against your souls! Despair not of the Mercy of GOD for GOD forgives all sins. He is OFT-FORGIVING, MOST MERCIFUL."
(Qur-ān xxxix. 53)

But as for any single verse whose English construction doesn't run counter its basic meaning, we do praise thereof the SUPREME HELPER and do we say after the Blessed[4]:

"And they shall say: **'Praise be to GOD, Who has guided us to this (felicity). Never could we have found guidance, had it not been for the Guidance of GOD.'"**

"And the end of their prayer will be:
'Praise be to GOD, the CHERISHER and SUSTAINER of the Worlds!
'"

---

[4] Qur-ān vii. 43 and x. 10

Transliteration of Arabic words and names

ا	a	ض	d̲
ب	b	ط	t̲
ت	t	ظ	z̲
ث	t̲h	ع	'
ج	j	غ	gh
ح	h̲	ف	f
خ	k̲h	ق	q
د	d	ک	k
ذ	dh	ل	l
ر	r	م	m
ز	z	ن	n
س	s	ه ة	h
ش	sh	و	w
ص	s̲	ي	y

Short Vowels		Long Vowels	
◌َ	a	ا	ã
◌ِ	i	ى	ĩ
◌ُ	u	و	ũ

However, we write sometimes some words in the spelling forms commonly accepted.

Glossary

Adab: Ethics which implies as well an idea of correctness with people as that of reverence of the Lord.

At-Ta<u>s</u>awwuf (Sufism): translated sometimes as "Muslim Mysticism", it describes schematically a trend of Muslim masters who theorize the purification of the heart and of the soul, so as to attain God's "Neighborhood".

Dhikr: remembrance of God and assiduous repetition of His Fine Names.

<u>H</u>*adīth:* maxim or story reported from the Prophet (PBH).

Ha<u>d</u>ratu-l-Lãh: God's "Neighborhood" the worshipper is aiming to attain.

Haqīqah: knowledge of deeper realities dealing with inner spiritual states and other mystical considerations.

Ijma': consensus of the doctors of Islamic law who adopt unanimously the same juridical award (*fatwa*) on a particular question.

<u>Kh</u>*ãdimu-r-Rasũli Lãh:* the Servant of the Prophet (PBH), the spiritual title of Sheikh Ahmadou Bamba.

Murĩd: GOD-seeker, disciple who aspires to get nearer the LORD under the guidance of a spiritual master (*Shay<u>kh</u>* or *Sheikh*); commonly the followers of Sheikh Ahmadou Bamba.

Murĩdiyya (or Muridism): The *tarĩqa* (brotherhood or order) founded by Sheikh Ahmadou Bamba.

Nãfila (plur.: *Nawãfil*): optional prayers which are strongly recommended by Islamic Law although their being not mandatory.

Rak'a: division of the prayer; most prayers are made up with 2 or 4 rak'a.

Salãt alã Nabĩ (plur.: *Salawãt*): Calling for Blessings upon the Prophet Muhammad (PBH).

Shari'a: Islamic law.

Sheikh: spiritual master (however when we say "the Sheikh" without any other particular we are referring to Sheikh Ahmadou Bamba).

Shirk: assigning partners to God Most High; the opposite of *Tawhĩd.*

Sũfi: who that puts into rigorous practice the principles of Sufism.

Sunnah: acts and maxims of the Prophet (PBH) any Muslim has to comply with.

Sũrah (plur. *Surã*): a chapter of the Qur-ãn.

Tarĩqa (plur. *Turũq*): Islamic brotherhood or Sufi order.

Tawhĩd: deep faith and certainty in God's Unity (also knowledge which deals with such a theme).

Wird: set of pleas, of Koranic verses and of various invocations any member of a *tarĩqa* (Sufi brotherhood) has to repeat a certain number of times everyday.

Contents

CHAPTER III: MUSLIM ETHICS (*Adab*) AND SOME BENEFICIAL PRACTICES OF WORSHIP (*Fadãil*)

IN THE NAME OF GOD, MOST GRACIOUS, MOST MERCIFUL

May GOD bestow His Peace and His Blessings upon our Master Muḥammad.

"Whoever expects to meet his LORD, let him work righteousness and, in the worship of his LORD, admit no partner"
(Qur-ãn xviii. 110)

GOD is my LORD and I assign Him no partner.

There is no Power, no Means but in Him.

O my LORD! Rank us amongst those who really fear Thee, those whose deeds Thou acceptest.

Never rank us among *"those whose efforts have been wasted in this life, while they thought that they were acquiring good by their works"* (Qur-ãn xviii. 104).

And deprive not us of the reward of this versified work or that of any other deed, by the name of our Noble Master Muḥammad,

May he be granted Peace and Blessings.

Foreword

IN THE NAME OF GOD, MOST GRACIOUS, MOST MERCIFUL

1- As an [humble servant] named **Ahmad Al-Mbackiyu,** and as the disciple of my father[5] - *may GOD, the ETERNAL ABSOLUTE, let him enter the loftiest Paradise*

2- *...In the company of any sincere Muslim and all who profess that worship must exclusively be devoted to the Only GOD - Amen*

3- I begin in praising GOD, Who requires from us genuine deeds and compliance with the rules of Ethics (*Adab*)[6],

4- He Who looks at our inner heart and at our spiritual qualities but not at our mere external appearances

5- Then be Peace and Blessings upon [the Prophet] who that shall intercede for us in the Hereafter,

6- Who that is adorned with the virtues of rectitude and that is free from any peril-leading vice:

7- ...[The Holy Messenger named] **Muhammad,** who has relieved us of pain. [May such Peace and Blessings be granted as well] to his Family, his Companions and all the Muslim Community

---

[5] Until his father's death - during the month of *Muharram* 1300 h. (1882-83) - the Sheikh Ahmadu Bamba considered himself and behaved strictly as the humble disciple of his father who taught him in the past. So had he the habit to introduce himself in such terms in all the books he composed during their coexistence and during the period succeeding his father's death.

[6] The word *Adab* (Ethics) implies, in Mystics' language, as well an idea of politeness and *savoir-vivre* with people as an idea of reverence and "propriety" vis-à-vis the LORD through our everyday attitude (*Cf.* Chapter III); what are considered by Sufis as the highest standards of real « ethics »..

8- And may that so be as long as any who strives hard against Satan, his basic drives and his lust will gain one day [right to dwell aye in] Heaven

9- And as long as whosoever endeavours to cleanse his soul of any vice will gain Divine Light and achieve GOD's Satisfaction

10- And as long as any who devotes not himself entirely to this present life will get closer to GOD, the Ultimate Truth

11- Thereupon, do know that the Science of GOD's Unity (At-Taw*h*īd) may be divided into two sorts; so does it exist two kinds of Taw*h*īd

12- * The first one is just verbal, consisting in a oral profession of faith
     * Whereas the second one consists in true knowledge [of GOD's Attributes] and in deep understanding[7]

13- The first sort is quite widespread [among believers] whilst the second one is reserved [to just few chosen people]

14- As regards that which is widespread we have already consecrated thereto a previous work put into verses[8]

---

[7] For the Masters a distinction has to be made between (1) the profession of GOD's Unity uttered by the common of Believers and (2) that of the Elite of the True Knowers which results from their factual experience of the unique basis of the Creation.

[8] This is a reference to a former book called Mawāhibu-l-Qudūs (The Gifts granted by [GOD], the HOLY ONE) consecrated by the Sheikh to the basic elements of theology any Muslim has to know.

15- [Taking up in fact] a former book written in prose by As-Sanūsī, a great-grand-son of the Messenger

16- *May GOD be Satisfied with [As-Sanūsī] and impart to [the Prophet] Peace and Blessings as great as the number of existing creatures-*

17- As regarding that which is reserved [to the Elite], we are going to devote this present versified work thereto

18-[Nonetheless do realize that] the Virtuous [Masters] have already written thereof books of merit which are all endowed with secrets [of benefit]

19-Such as our Sheikh, the renowned Regenerator [of Islam], the Great Imam Al-Ghazāli[9], such as the Eminent Ibn 'Ata Lāh

20-Such as our Master Sīdi Mukhtār, related to the Kuntiyu family, who that is endowed with Pure Lights, the *Ghawth* [10] of the creatures, the Eminent *Qutb,*

21- Such as our Sheikh named Muhammad [Kuntiyu], the Caliph leant on the Truth coming from the LORD of the creatures

22- Such as our Sheikh Muhammad, related to the Deymani tribe, the great commentator of the Qur-ān

23- And others amongst the honorable Masters- *may GOD gather us with them on the Resurrection Day-*

---

[9] For information about the authors mentioned by the *Sheikh,* refer to the biographical annex (Tome IV, at www.majalis.org/masalik).

[10] The notion of *Ghawth* (Supreme Rescuer) and that of *Qutb* (Spiritual Pole) are closely connected with the technical vocabulary of *Tasawwuf* (Muslim Mystics). Each period is spiritually under the leadership of a Saint (*Ghawth*) assisted by another Saint (*Qutb*) chosen among the August Congregation of Godly Men. These Spiritual Degrees may be held concurrently.

24- Nevertheless their works, due in part to their voluminous sizes, are neglected by most of the people of this generation

25- As for me, I have chosen to put in verse Al-Yadālī's prose book [The Seal of Sufism] relying only on the Help of GOD, the SUPREME HELPER

26- Because that book embodies verily the *Seal of Sufism* inasmuch as it gathers everything that has been written previously by the Virtuous Ancients thereon

27- I composed thereof a work which contains remedies for any such whose heart has been dulled by earthly lusts [so as to make it spiritually ill]

28- ...And verses which enable to improve the spiritual state of any novice or even experienced person, naturally if he is not filled with jealousy

29- For an envious person shall never profit from the advantages imparted to his contemporary and never shall he follow him

30- And nothing would ever rejoice him but learning that latter's sudden death!

31- *May GOD protect us from a jealous and from any evil caused by an enemy filled with hatred or by a denier*

32- I have revived in this book the lights of knowledge people have rendered dead letter in their errant ignorance

33- Hoping to be granted as a reward, for my brother Al-Yadālī and I, lofty degrees in Paradise

34- Therewith, I do solicit prayers from all who will cast their eyes over [our book], or that will leaf through it and mostly from any who will read it [entirely]

35- May any that will cast a glance over it intend for us the Most Excellent Prayers ever been meant for a servant

36- For prayers are, of a certain, beneficial as well to the dead in the grave as to the living and [there is no doubt about their] entailing Reward

37- I have entitled this book *"Masāliku-l-Jinān"* (**WAYS UNTO HEAVEN"**) based on Al-Deymani's[11] prose work "

38- Because I put in verse here everything Al-Deymani has made mention of in his book called *Khātimatu-t-Taṣawwuf* (The Seal of Sufism)

39- And I have drawn afterwards further useful complements liable to enhance the merit of [The Seal of Sufism] from another book entitled *A-Dhahabu-l-Ibrīz* (The Pure Gold)[12]

40- I have also happened to add other developments quoted from other books different from both of these so as to supplement their contents

---

[11] The Sheikh happens sometimes to mention Al-Yadālī under the name of *Al-Deymani* (the member of the Deyman tribe) according to the habit consisting in assigning a person the name of his tribe or people.

[12] This book has not to be mistaken, as did Fernand Dumond in La Pensée Religieuse d'Amadou Bamba (Nouvelles Editions Africaines, Dakar 1975), with another book entitled *Kitab-al-Ibriz min Kalam Sayd 'Abd-al-'Aziz Al-Dabbagh*. This latter was written in 1119 h (about 1709) by Aḥmad ibn Al Mubarak a Moroccan disciple of the prestigious 'Abd-al-'Aziz Al-Dabbagh, a Saint belonging to the Tijāni *tarīqa*. That book was known as the "livre de chevet" of the West-African *Tijāni*. As for *A-Dhahabu-l-Ibrīz* (The Pure Gold) it was written by Al-Yadālī.

41- Such as *Iḥyā Ulūmi-d-Dīn* (Enlivening Religious Knowledge) [by the famous Imam Al-Ghazāli] and *Junatu-l-Murīd* (The Shield of the GOD-seeker) of our eminent Master [Sīdi Mukhtār Kuntiyu]

42- Therein whenever I shall happen to write *"he said"* with no further particulars do infer that I am quoting Al-Ghazāli, the famous [Master]

43- But as regarding [quotations from] any other author amongst these Noble Sheikhs, I shall mention explicitly his name

44- And whenever you see the phrase *"I say"*, do know that it would be an inference I have drawn from their texts

45- Thence everything that is in this book is authentic; so have faith in it and do follow its recommendations

46- And may not my low renown in this generation[13] divert thee from giving credit to this pious deed!

47- And never be dissuaded from holding this book in due regard by my belonging to the black race

48- For [as quoted from the Book] the most honorable human being before GOD is who that fears HIM the most, without any possible doubt,[14]

49- So black skin does not imply insanity or ill understanding

50- O thou that art shrewd! Never neglect my verses on the [alleged] pretence that I do not apply their contents

---

[13] During that period, the young Sheikh had not yet gained his tremendous fame.

[14] *Cf.* Qur-ān xlix. 13: *"Verily the most honoured of you in the sight of GOD is (he who is) the most righteous of you."*

51-And do not grant the Virtuous Ancients the exclusive prerogative of the Favors bestowed by GOD - *wouldst thou then be led astray*

52- For it happens sometimes that a man living in *modern times* know secrets which were ignored by men living in *ancient times*

53-As goes the saying: *"Drizzle may well precede pouring rain, however pouring rain is far better to the crops than drizzle"*

54- O thou that art scorning my work! Do call to thy remembrance this Prophetic maxim (*ḥadith*): ***"My community is like a rain, [no one knoweth which part thereof is the best; the first part or the last part]"***

55- I have composed these verses in the sole order to serve my Muslim Brethren, hoping to obtain thereby the Satisfaction of GOD, the MOST GRACIOUS

56- And that is solely from GOD, my LORD, I solicit to accept my pious deeds and from Whom I seek the favour to attain my aim - HE is verily the MOST BOUNTIFUL LORD!

57- I also beseech HIM to grant His Oft-forgiveness, His Compassion and His Mercy to the entire Muslim Community, in the life here below as in the Hereafter

58- I do hope that HE will lead unto guidance any who reads this work - *HE is verily the MAJESTIC LORD Who holds grace for His devotees*

59- I also expect from HIM the favor of making these verses a shield from Blame for all their readers

60- And that this book may entail for us, once in the grave, Salvation from its trials and from the Panic of the Great Gathering Day

61- And that it bring to us, by Heavenly Mercy, the two Lights of the two Houses[15]

62- May also the MOST HIGH enhance our uprightness, our spiritual knowledge and our benefits through its recommendations

63- And that is solely with HIM I do seek safeguard from shortcomings and from Blame

64- And I hope from HIM the Fortitude to always act in conformity with the Tradition (*Sunnah*) of the Elected Messenger, the Best one in adoring the LORD

65- *May GOD impart Him Peace and Blessings as well as his Family, his Companions and all that have followed his footpath*

66- We seek refuge in GOD, in the name of [Mu<u>h</u>ammad], the Head of the Prophets, from the mischief of Satan, the Head of the damned

67- We seek His Safeguard from any rebelling creature and from the *"mischief of the envious as he practises envy"* (Qur-ãn cxiii. 5)

68- We ask for His Protection from any sort of evil stemming from man's eye or man's tongue and from any harmful creature

69- From the MAJESTIC LORD that grants complete Satisfaction to any who makes longingly his way towards Him

70- ...I do solicit Salvation for any such that will read our book or that will meditate on its content

71- ...And for any that will acquire it, either in possession or through renting, and for any that will write it out or that will borrow it

---

[15]GOD's Guidance in this world and, in the Next Life, the Light provided to the Believers and about which the Qur-ãn teaches (lxvi. 8): " *Their light will run forward before them and by their right hands (...)* "

72- [I beseech my LORD for this] in the name of our Beloved Prophet Ahmad, the Accredited Intercessor - *may Peace and Blessings be ensured, for aye, to him*

73- *...As to his Family, his Companions and all that will follow in his in his footsteps until the Day of Trials*

74- This work is made up with three main chapters preceded by a preamble; they have, nonetheless, to be considered altogether [as forming a whole]

75- ✍The first chapter is devoted to the creatures and their respective relations with [GOD], enumerated and thoroughly examined [by the Masters]

76- ✍The next one goes into human vices, those which are discernible or hidden, wherever they may be found

77- ✍The third chapter deals with the rules of Ethics (*Adab*) and some beneficial practices of worship

78- Now that is time to enter the heart of the matter and, for such a purpose, GOD's Assistance do we beseech

79- So - after having first said the *Basmalah*[16], rendered thanks to GOD, asked for Blessings upon the Prophet and testified that *"There is no Power, no Means but in GOD"* - do we say this

---

[16]The phrase *"Bismi-Lāhi Rahmāni Rahīmi"* (In the Name of GOD, MOST GRACIOUS, MOST MERCIFUL) any Muslim is recommended to say before any action or undertaking.

Preamble

Preamble

80- According to the Masters, religious knowledge is divided into two kinds:
> - Exoteric knowledge (*'Ilm Ẕāhir*)
> - Esoteric knowledge (*'Ilm Bāṭin*)

81- Exoteric knowledge is in charge of improving human actions while esoteric knowledge deals with human spiritual moods and degrees

82- The first one is known under the name of *Fiqh* [Islamic Law] whilst the second one is called *Taṣawwuf* [Sufism]

83- It behoves to any believer to comply first with the Rules of *Fiqh* prior to practising *Taṣawwuf*

84- Thence whosoever disregards the Legal Rules of Worship (*Fiqh*) [and undertakes the practising of *Taṣawwuf*] shall perish in this world by the sentence of the Doctors of the Law[17]

85- Any such who neglects the inner aspects of religion (*Taṣawwuf*) shall perish in the Next World by the Will of the MAJESTIC LORD

---

[17]This concerns specially *Sūfis* who attained indefinable spiritual states so much so they gave up the Legal Rules of worship; the reason why public Islamic authorities had in the past to put them to death according to the Law. Refer to the famous case of the Mystic Mansur Al-Hajj (about 858-922), an ancient disciple of Al-Junayd, who turned away from Mystics' classical teachings and who undertook a life of wanderer between Persian provinces, preaching Love for GOD. Maintaining mystical junction with the LORD, he proclaimed publicly "I am the Truth!" (*Anna Al-Haqq*), which was considered as an usurpation of GOD's Supreme Power (*Shirk*), reason for which he was put into death by public authorities after 8-years' detention.

86- So it is considered as compulsory for any servant to combine respect for the established Rules of Worship [*Fiqh*] with concern for inner aspects [*Taṣawwuf*] so as to obtain reward

87- Know thou that who that conforms to the apparent modes of worship whilst giving no credit to inwardly considerations is assuredly a thorough rascal!

88- As for who that does quite the reverse [focusing on inner aspects so as to deny any importance to the external rules of worship], his case is ranked among the heretics'

89- But as regards who that succeeds in combining both of them [*Fiqh* and *Taṣawwuf*], that is a fine model [of balance] thou hast to pattern thyself upon

90- This award has been passed by the Imam Mãlik[18] - *may [GOD], the ABSOLUTE SOVEREIGN* (Al-Mãlik) *impart him Mercy and be Satisfied with him*

91- Do know that knowledge and action (or theory and practice) are both the way unto Bliss, yea!

92- So devote resolutely thyself to both of them, do cleanse thyself of any failing and remain in absolute purity (*Ikhlãs*)

93- Endeavour to always conforming to [seeking for godly knowledge and to putting it into practice], in sincerity and pure-heartedness - so shalt thou gain fine qualities

---

[18]The Imam Mãlik ibn Anas (94-179 H.) was one of the four great founders of *Madhhãb* (Islamic Juridical Schools) inasmuch as he founded the Madinah Juridical School called also the *Malikite* School in which belongs Sheikh Aḥmadu Bamba.

94- ...And shalt be ranked amongst those who follow the Tradition of the Chosen [Prophet] - *be upon him Peace and Blessings from [GOD], the MAKER of the earth and the heavens*

95- *...As upon his Family, his Companions and all that are following in their footsteps and are taking them as models*

96- Be thou steadfast in always fulfilling the hard actions relating to [knowledge and its putting into practice] and do flee from laziness!

97- Behave as thou wouldst do if thou knew that thy death was impending - as recommended [by the Holy Prophet]

98- If, in accomplishing such two principles, thou bear patiently the hardships befalling on thee during the short stay thou wilt spend on earth

99- ...Shalt thou, o my Dear Fellow!, obtain Salvation and dwell for aye in the Garden of Delight

100- Know however that far-reaching knowledge with many actions of worship while one is full of shortcomings [constitute an delusion]

101- However giving up both of them lest one should have one's effort besmirched by [unavoidable] failings, or their [absented-mindly] fulfilment without any true reverence in the heart, are among the most dangerous illusions

102- As for delaying one's repentance, lest one should relapse into similar sins, that is naught but a Snare of Satan, the Rebel

103- Do know, o my Brother!, that knowledge prevails over action, being its principle and root - *bliss to whom is endowed with it!*

104- Nevertheless, knowledge could not bear fruit and bring profit without its subsequent putting into practice; so try to combine both of them

105- Few actions based on definite knowledge will, of a surety, entail more Reward than a host of actions performed with ignorance

106- Useful knowledge [in the Hereafter] is just that which has been learnt and taught for the Sole Countenance of the MAJESTIC LORD, the ONE

107- But not that which has been learnt for superficial debates, making parade and searching for glamour[19] - *know thou this!*

108- Nor that which has been acquired for worldly purposes as the liking for authority and high responsibilities

109- Nor that which has been got in order to fill people's hearts with admiration -*think thou about*

110- Whosoever makes a great effort to acquire [religious] knowledge for just such kinds of worldly purposes

111- ...And who repents not thereof before his death or his old age, and who tries not hard to make up for his errors of youth,

112- ...That one shall get, on the Day of Questioning and Reckoning, naught but Misfortune, Blame and Chastisement!

113- For his vast knowledge will become an argument against him on that Day; one has verily to fear such an argument

114- Useful knowledge is that which fills its bearer with Fear (*Taqwā*) of GOD, the CREATOR of the servants

---

[19]*Cf.* Qur-ān xl. 56: "*Those who dispute about the Signs of GOD without any authority bestowed on them, -there is nothing in their breasts but (the quest of) greatness, which they shall never attain to. Seek refuge, then, in GOD: it is He Who hears and sees (all things).*" Qur-ān vi. 68: "*When thou seest men engaged in vain discourse about Our Signs, turn away from them unless they turn to a different theme. If Satan ever makes thee forget, then after recollection, sit not thou in the company of those who do wrong.*"

115- That which inspires humility, asceticism, Ethics (*Adab*), self-effacement and the awareness of one's weakness [before GOD]

116- That which purifies the heart, helps in mastering the soul and prevents man from transgressing the Orders of the MAKER

117- As for such knowledge that has not theses virtues, it can save no one from our LORD's Hell, yea!

118- Best [religious] knowledge is indisputably that which treats of Theology and GOD's Unity (*'Ilm Tawḥīd*)

119- Come afterwards the Exegesis of the Qur-ān (*Tafsīru-l-Qur-ān*) and the Science of Prophetic Tradition (*Ḥadīth*) - *as conveyed by Al-Daymānī*

120- After these three [main disciplines] come Islamic Law (*Fiqh*)

121- ...And literary sciences serving as tools for these chief disciplines

122- Such as grammar, prosody, rhetoric, language and the like

123- The best deed one may performed is assuredly that which is liable to entail the most widely spread profit [to society] like knowledge

124- ...Which helps in removing ignorance and in keeping men far off mischief and which, moreover, is beneficial to any upright person

125- Or any action that helps to purify the heart, as trifling as it may appear, provided it is regularly and firmly accomplished - *so put it the Wise*

126- Or any act which is hard-doing for the Soul - as spending money [in GOD's Cause] for any miserly person

127- As fasting for the greedy one or discretion and good deeds concealment for any who is eager for celebrity and praises

128- The worst transgression is, most certainly, that which hardens the heart and makes it forget GOD's worship

129- The best *Dhikr* [GOD's Remembrance] a servant can perform is reading meditatively and thoroughly GOD's Holy Book [the Qur-ān]

130- A single verse read with thoughtfulness is indeed more beneficial than the heedless reading of the entire Book

131- And little does it matter that [such a reflective reading] is made during a prayer or with the Text before one's eyes, were it in a low or in a loud voice – [this last mode is however preferred] if one feels safe from ostentation[20]

132- Performance of *Nawāfil* (optional prayers) indoors is also credited with well-renowned advantages, mostly those accomplished in the night, particularly during its last part[21]

133- [O my Brother! know that] the greatest wish of the dead is coming back to life

134- ...So as to spend on earth were it only the slightest lapse of time and to perform a single good deed liable to entail some benefit for them once back to the Hereafter[22]

---

[20] *Cf.* verses 306-316.

[21] Night is traditionally divided into three parts; its last third is here implied.

[22] *Cf.* Qur-ān lxxxix. 21-24: *"Nay! When the earth is pounded to powder, and thy LORD cometh, and His angels, rank upon rank, and Hell, that Day, is brought (face to face), -on that Day will man remember, but how will that remembrance profit him? He will say:* "Ah! Would that I had sent forth (good deeds) for my (future) life!"

135- Thence do make the most of the rest of thy life, regretting past times [misused in trivialities] without adoring GOD, and race thou towards good deeds before it become too late!

136- Forget not to improve thy inmost heart [in keeping a watchful eye on thy defects]

137- Strive thou, o Dear Brother!, in always mastering thy senses and be among "those who take care of their breath"

138- For any time [as brief as] a human breath will be worth a precious jewel

139- ...With which one would be able to buy a Wondrous and Eternal Treasure [on the Last Day] - *wake thou up!*

140- Losing such a time without adoring [GOD] shall entail great loss on the Last Hour

141- But if ever thou spend it in transgressing [the Heavenly Orders], that is an irretrievable disaster - *do know it*

142/144- So devote thyself in reviving thy lifetime with
- Due fulfilment of Canonical Obligations (*Farāīḏ*) out of any heedlessness
- Accomplishment of voluntary deeds (*Nawāfil*)
- Regular fasting
- Wird[23] daily practice
- Remembrance and utterance of GOD's Holy Names (*Dhikr*)[24]
- Meditation on GOD's Signs (*Fikr*)[25]

---

[23]Practice consisting in regular repetition of a set of gathered verses and pleas taken from the Book and from other accredited sources (*Cf.* chapter devoted to *wird* (v. 267-298)).

[24]Practice consisting in repeating in reverence one of GOD's numerous Fine Names (*Asmāu-l-Ḥusnā*) or other phrases of Glorification, of Praise and so (*Cf.* chapter devoted to *zikr* (v.299-408)).

[25] *Cf.* verses 409-461.

- Spending in alms and in aid for the needy, just for the Satisfaction of [GOD], the SUPREME PROTECTOR

145-[Always perform good deeds], especially on the Favourite Days[26], in favour of thy kin and for the Men of Merit

146- Persevere in always acting with good intentions and never be weary thereof

147- Is likewise [held as valuable] conveying good tidings and joy to our fellow Muslims but not bad news or evil

148- Keep for thyself provisions [for Future Life] in regularly practising one of the accredited *wird*

149- ...Were it little, likely to be of some benefit for thee on the Day of Distress and Sorrow

150- Do make a point of performing it in purity and in discretion, without people knowing[27] - so wilt thou be praised on the Day of Rewarding

151- For most of the pious deeds openly accomplished will not be meritorious enough on that Day once disclosed

---

[26]Friday , the Day of *Ashūrā* and so (*Cf.* verses 236-254).
[27]Lest one should give way to ostentation.

True Knowledge

[as] admonitions and complements taken from

"A-Dhahabu-l-Ibrĩz " (The Pure Gold) and from other

works

152- Satan, the Damned - I tell you - has deluded people; the reason why they continually concern themselves in only what will bring misfortune to them

153- They cease not seeking to know things devoid of any sort of benefit, neither in the grave nor during the Great Gathering of the Resurrection

154- They devote themselves to [worldly affairs] which are unable, on the Day of Anguish and Affliction, to ward off the Hellish Chastisement; they entirely throw themselves into heedlessness and pleasures

155- Is not any knowledge useful and - thence - all "learned" persons are not comparable

156- There are certain kinds of knowledge which harden the heart, which entail pride and the forgetting of the LORD

157- So will be amongst the "learned" persons many who will receive as a reward Tomorrow naught but ruin and reprimanding!

158- We may read [in this instance] in some Al-Hilālī's poem - *may GOD, that Who holds all Majesty, be Satisfied with him -*

159- *"True knowledge is that which fills the heart with Fear of GOD, the ALL-KNOWER; any that is not endowed with such knowledge is a blameworthy ignoramus, of a certain!"*

160- Will not be of any benefit - I tell you - such knowledge which has been learnt for the sole sake of being continually admired and praised by people

161- The same for that which has been acquired just for competition and rivalry - as a Pharisee would do

162- [Useful knowledge is] neither that which has been learnt [in order to be consecrated *Mufti*] so as to rush at *Fatwas* (juridical opinions) and awards likely to cause harm

163- Nor that which has been searched in aiming thereby to enslave one's brethren

164- Or knowledge with which man spends his whole time in sport and amusement - *[weigh ye up the relevance of these remarks], o ye my Brethren!*

165- Or that which fills the heart with envy, resentment, arrogance and going astray

166- Or that which incites unto animosity, controversies and endless verbal sparring

167- Or that which prompts unto presumptuousness, self-praising and aggressiveness

168- Or that which leads unto quarrelling, quick-temperance, deceitfulness and struggling

169- Or that with which one is aiming earthly goods through hoarding and denying [to spend on GOD's Cause] or that which incites unto vain chattering

170- Nay! Nay! But useful knowledge is that which shows first one's own failings to any that is endowed with it

171- That which drives unto patience, generosity, kindness, purity of worship and sense of decency

172- That which leads unto loving the Truth, spiritual retreat, meditation, contemplation and thought

173- Such knowledge which instils fine spiritual virtues and other discernible qualities

174- Such knowledge which inspires fear of GOD and which prompts unto putting one's entire trust in HIM; that which incites unto asceticism, unto well-founded hope[28] and withdrawing often from society so as to devote one's time to the LORD

175- Such knowledge which leads out of excessive desires and out of relying on the creatures [disregarding so their Very *CREATOR*]

176- Such knowledge which cures from jealousy, arrogance, going astray, hatred and self-conceit

177- And which encourages unto assisting and maintaining good relationship with one's Muslim brethren for the Sole Countenance of the ETERNAL-ABSOLUTE

178- Indeed thus is the true nature of knowledge: either does it lead unto uprightness who that is endowed with it or shall it unavoidably lead him down towards profound perdition

179- [Al-Ghazāli] added that: *"Whosoever helps who that is seeking for knowledge, in his aim or in any of his worldly affairs,*

---

[28]Hope must be the right outcome of the effort made by a steadfast worshipper in GOD's Service, relying on His Infinite Mercy, but not a self-deluding feeling one cherishes without turning in the least aside from sinning...

180- *"...Will share with him aught he might be imparted as a reward, just the way any such that knowingly sells a sword to a brigand should be involved in the crimes perpetrated by this one."*

181- Knowledge does not consist in a great number of reports and quotations, nay! but that is a Pure Light brightening with true understanding the heart [of whom that is endowed with][29]

182- Thence do seek thereby the only Countenance of the MAJESTIC - o thou Dear Fellow! – so permanent delights shalt thou be granted

183- Indeed any who fears not the LORD of the Worlds is far from being "learned"; had he mastered all the branches of knowledge!

---

[29]*Cf.* Qur-ān viii. 29: "*O ye who believe! If ye fear GOD, He will grant you a Criterion (to judge between right and wrong)."*

Pieces of Wisdom

184- If thou ever persist in using the Sustenance provided by GOD while permanently disobeying HIM

185- ...And never repent thereof [and never seek steadfastly for His Forgiveness], shalt thou, of a surety, be thrown into Hell

186- Thence never commit in thy life the offence to always using the spiritual and material means of subsistence granted by GOD while adoring something else[30]

187- Do multiply instead thy good deeds for the only Sake of GOD, the ONE, [with a determination] corresponding to thy very need of His Assistance

188- And act thou for this present world just according to the [short] stay thou wilst dwell therein - o thou that art clear-minded!

189- And act thou for the Future World according to the [eternal] sojourn thou wilst abide therein; whosoever distorts this principle is, of a surety, done for

190- Do act with a view to GOD's Hell [in resisting temptations] with a patience and a resistance as great as it would be weak in withstanding its dreadful heat once thrown therein[31]
191- If thou fear duly thy LORD, the ONE, any other creature will fear thee, just owing to such GOD-fearingness

---

[30]Indeed anything, besides GOD MOST HIGH, whose love or fear fills man's heart so as to divert him from His Remembrance, is somehow adored: intermediaries, idols, creatures, lust and so.
[31]Knowing that human weakness cannot in the least be put in relation with the nightmarish Fury of Hell, there is no question of withstanding its Violence -were it during the slightest while. Thence, in accordance with such a lack of forbearance, man must bear in this world patience inversely proportional.

Meditation

(Fikr)

409- Meditation is ranked amongst the most valuable occupation, if frequently practised[32]

410- [Al-Ghazalī] said in "*Ihyā 'Ulūmi-d-Dīn*"(The Revival of Religious Sciences) - *do bear in mind this quotation of his:*"**The most admirable fruits religious practice can yield in this present world are**

411- *...the acquiring of* **Ma'rifa** (*True Knowledge of the LORD*) *and of* **Uns** (*the feeling of Intimacy with GOD*) *deriving from* **Dhikr** *practice*

412- *Do know that such feeling to live in constant Neighbourhood with* **GOD** (**Uns**) *is achieved through regular practice of* **Dhikr,** *whilst True Knowledge* (**Ma'rifa**) *is acquired through continuous meditation* (**Fikr**)"

413- It has been also said that a single hour of profound meditation [on GOD's Signs] is better than a whole year of adoration [without meditation] - *thence do combine both of them*

414- Know that meditation is the most genuine mirror for any who believes truly in the MOST GRACIOUS

415- Because that is through *Fikr* practice man can gaze forthrightly at himself and can discern his good deeds - to which he will be delight - as well as his shortcomings -[he will have to put right]-

---

[32]*Cf.* Qur-ān iii. 190-191:"*Behold! In the creation of the heavens and the earth, and the alternation of Night and Day, -there are indeed Signs for men to understand, - Men who remember GOD standing, sitting, and lying down on their sides, and contemplate the (wonders of) creation in the heavens and the earth, (with the saying):* "Our LORD not for naught hast Thou created (all) this! Glory to Thee! Give us salvation from the Chastisement of the Fire..."""

416- Such self-fairness is a required quality for any servant that is seeking for Loftiness from our MOST GRACIOUS LORD - *How MAJESTIC and ELEVATED He is! -*

417- The fruit of meditation is admittance in GOD's Neighbourhood (*Hadratu-l-Lāh*) for he that has already got true Knowledge (*Ma'rifa*)

418- As regarding the meditation of the ascetics, it concerns the fading of this world and the flickeness of its affairs

419- Such a practice strengthens their determination and gives them enough heart to stand upright and to turn their backs on wordly trivialities

420- As for the [common] worshippers' meditation, it relates to the marvellous Reward promised by GOD [to His devotees] and to the countless Advantages [procured by His Adoration]

421- ...Which augments their longing for worshipping and makes stronger their ardour thereto

422- Concerning the meditation of the True Knowers (*'ārifīn*) on the Gratification and the Delights emanating from the MAKER of the sky

423- ...That adds to their Love for GOD - *Real Grandeur belongs indeed to the LORD of the creatures!*

424- [We hold from] Ibn Abī Jamrah, the Champion of Piety - *may GOD be eternally Satisfied with him-*

425- ...That unremitting meditation is the best occupation a Believer can spend his time on
426- Because man can get sound and discriminating knowledge only in exercising regularly his reflexive reason in meditation

427- Likewise faith will not be firm and perfectly sincere until it is upheld by frequent meditation - this opinion is unanimously accepted

428- O Dear Brethren! Know that the kind of genuine faith and certainty following upon meditation

429- ...Is not similar to spontaneous and intuitive belief [of ordinary people] - the first is indeed more perfect

430- It has been reported - and there is no divergence about - that a single while of deep thought [on Heavenly Realities] is far more valuable than endless acts of worship [with no actual meditation]

431- Such a preference is due to the fact that man's faith gains in vigour whenever he meditates

432- Because the Divine Truth will thus appear crystal-clearly to him and, fully convinced about Higher Realities, he will be able to foster his pure-heartedness and gain more spiritual stability

433- The vitality of thy faith reposes on the deepening of thy thoughts, o Dear Brother

434- Keep on thy gaze at the "mirror" of meditation, in withdrawing often from people for many hours

435- So the Truth will appear to thee, o my Friend! - Is it not in this way [the Prophet Abraham], GOD's Friend, acquired his conviction [about the necessary existence of a Being transcending materiality]?[33]

---

[33]In Qur-ān vi. 75-79: "*So did We show Abraham the kingdom of the Heavens and the earth, that he might have certitude. When the night covered him over, he saw a star; he said:* "This is my LORD." *But when it set, he said:* "I love not those that set". *When he saw the moon rising in splendour, he said:* ":"This is my LORD." *But when the moon set, he said:* "Unless my LORD guide me, I shall surely be among those who go astray". *When he saw the sun rising (in splendour,) he said:* "This is my LORD; this is the greatest (of all)." *But when the sun set, he said:* "O my people! I am free from your (guilt) of giving partners to GOD. For me,

436- *May the most excellent Peace, from the LOFTY ONE, be bestowed on the Beloved Prophet [Mu__h__ammad], on Abraham and on all their peers-*

437- Man can gain from a single hour of meditation [what will be highly beneficial] as far as his faith is concerned

438- ...And what he could not obtain in spending his whole lifetime in worshipping [unmeditatively]

439- Through deep meditation will distinctly come to the view the Way towards Religion - as wrote it the Sound Master

440- I am referring to Ibn Sa'īd, the keen mind related to the Deymān family - *may the MOST GRACIOUS be Satisfied with him for aye-*

441- It has been once asked to a saintly man: "**What gives thee such an [acute] knowledge of thy LORD?**"

442- He replied: "**I know HIM [through meditation which has enabled me] to grasp how disconcerting His manner to thwart our best arranged plans is!** "- *do meditate and so wilt thou prosper*

443- The best themes a servant can meditate on are assuredly the earth and the skies - as reported

444- Then comes reflection about the Favours [granted by GOD] because of its breeding grateful love for the BENEFACTOR

445- Thinking about the Fine Reward held in store for the Believers [in Paradise] enhances our longing for adoring GOD
446- ...And incites us unto increasing our efforts thereto; *this is actually profitable to a servant*

I have set my face, firmly and truly towards Him Who created the heavens and the earth, and never shall I give partners to GOD ""

447- Thinking about the Dreadful Chastisement in Hell, which threatens the wrongdoers, prompts us unto reforming

448- ...And increases our fear; so does it prevent man from relapsing into sinning - *what a beneficial outcome!*

449- Thinking about the Divine Kindness, which is hiding our failings before people, helps in always confiding in GOD's Nobleness

450- As it increases our hope and our reliance on His Assistance

451- Thou art also advised to study first and to meditate frequently on *what* has been created, nay on the Essence of *Who* has created[34]
452- Think not too much over thy material poverty, for that would overwhelm thee with distress and sorrow

---

[34] In Islamic Theology it is indeed recommended to reflect about GOD's Attributes, as one may perceive their manifold Manifestations in the Universe, but as far His True Essence is concerned Believers are advised to avoid meditating *too far*, for never will human reason succeed in grasping perfectly Who that has created it. *Cf.* Qur-ān v. 101-102: " *O ye who believe! Ask not questions about things which, if made plain to you, may cause you trouble. But if ye ask about things when the Qur-ān is being revealed, they will be made plain to you, GOD will forgive those: for GOD is OFT-FORGIVING, MOST FORBEARING. Some people before you did ask such questions, and on that account lost their faith. "* We found very instructive the commentary of these verses by Yusuf Ali: " *Many secrets are wisely hidden from us. If the future were known to us, we will not necessarily be happy. In many cases we should be miserable. If the inner meaning of some of the things we see before our eyes were disclosed to us, it might cause a lot of mischief. GOD's Message, in so far as it is necessary for shaping our conduct, is plain and open to us. But there are many things too deep for us to understand, either individually or collectively. It would be foolish to pry into them, as some people tried to do in the time of the Prophet. Where a matter is mentioned in the Qur-ān, we can reverently ask for its meaning. That is not forbidden. But we should never pass the bounds of (1) our own capacity to understand, (2) the time and occasion when we ask questions, and (3) the part of the Universal Plan which it is GOD's purpose to reveal to us. "*

453- Neither meditate on an injustice committed against thee by an unfair person, for that would increase the hatred and the anger between you – *do bear patience*

454- Do not [make endless plans for the future], leaning on thy hypothetical long life, for that will lead thee to prejudicial hoarding

455- [Such a reckless comportment], if persisting, will lead thee unto the irretrievable waste of thy lifetime and will incite thee unto postponing permanently thy resolution to worship duly the LORD

456- Do know that man can attain real disregard for earthly matters and true self-restraint only if he devotes steadily himself to empty any falsity out of his heart

457- Indeed, the toughest *Jihād* (Holy War) consists in hindering one's mind from ever involving in aught that is not proper

458- This is indeed most arduous; but any who trains not himself to such self-constraint outside the time of prayer will not either succeed thereto during his prayer[35]

459/460- O Dear Friend of mine! Persevere in meditating on [GOD's Signs through the Creation[36]]: the earth, the sky, the stars, the sun, the moon, the trees, water, fire, the hills

461- ...And other divine phenomena as day and night- so thy heart wilt be brightened by the lights of True Knowledge and Certainty!

---

[35] This means that if the servant wants to keep fully gathered during his prayer, he has to take the habit to meditating *outside* prayer time so as to train his mind in contemplating GOD at any time...

[36]*Cf.* Qur-ān xxii. 18:"*Seest thou not that to GOD prostrate all things that are in the heavens and on earth, - the sun, the moon, the stars; the hills, the trees, the animals; and a great number among mankind?...*"

Muslim Fraternity

Charity, consolidation of social bonds and other generous attitudes between muslims

462- As regards spending on charity (*Sadaqāt*)[37] and for GOD's Cause (*Infāq*), they encompass all the good things

463- Anything that can benefit a Muslim or any effort made to strengthen one's kinship bonds [are also highly valuable]

464- It has been said that, on the Day of Reckoning, when *Sirāt* Bridge will be thrown over Hell

465- ...And when the creatures will restlessly stir into sorrow and anguish [in waiting for their judgement], a Herald will suddenly call out: "***Where are those who kept on assisting Muslims?***"

---

[37]About Charity the Qur-ān teaches us (ii. 270-274): "*And whatever ye spend in charity or whatever vow you make, be sure GOD knows it all. But the wrongdoers have no helpers. If ye disclose (acts of) charity, even so it is well, but if ye conceal them, and make them reach those (really) in need, that is best for you: it will remove from you some of your (stains of) evil. And GOD is Well Acquainted with what ye do. It is nor for you to guide them to the Right Path, but GOD guides to the Right Path whom He pleaseth. Whatever of good ye give benefits your own souls, and ye shall only do so seeking the 'Face' of GOD. Whatever good ye give, shall be rendered back to you, and ye shall not be dealt unjustly. (Charity is) for those in need, who, in GOD's Cause are restricted (from travel) and cannot move about in the land, seeking (for trade or work): the ignorant man thinks, because of their modesty, that they are free from want. Thou shalt know them by their (unfailing) mark: they beg not importunately from all and sundry. And whatever of good ye give, be assured GOD knoweth it well. Those who (in charity) spend of their goods by night and by day, in secret and in public, have their reward with their LORD: on them shall be no fear, nor shall they grieve.*" Refer also to a *Hadith Qudsi* related by Abu Harayrah (may God be pleased with him) from the Prophet (PBUH), who said: "*God (mighty and sublime be He) said: Spend (on charity), O son of Adam, and I shall spend on you.*"

466- All who will be concerned will reply together: "*Here we are!*"; then they will be ordered to enter forthwith in Paradise

467- ...In telling them: "*Enter ye all in Heaven, without any pain or hardship*"

468- So be always helpful with all thy Muslim Brethren for the Sole Countenance of GOD out of any hurtful remark, and do persevere thereto

469- Do also conceal kindly [aught that relates to them] and which is liable to be unsightly[38]; but as for anything that is likely to content them, display thou it

470- And to all who come to thee in quest of help, provide them plentifully with gifts, if thou art wealthy

471- But descend not to continually hoarding money for fear of poverty!

---

[38]Concerning the necessity to preserve the moral integrity of our Muslim Brothers and Sisters, refer to the story of the slander of our Mother Ha*d*rat 'Aisha (the Prophet's wife) and the harangue of the Qur-ān thereon (xxiv. 12-20): "*Why did not the Believers -men and women- when ye heard of the affair, thought well of their people and say, "This (charge) is an obvious lie"?(...) Were it not for the Grace and mercy of GOD on you, in this world and the hereafter, a grievous chastisement would have seized you in that ye rushed glibly into this affair. Behold, ye receive it on your tongues, and said out of your mouths things of which ye had no knowledge; and ye thought it to be a light matter, while it was most serious in the sight of GOD. And why did ye not, when ye heard it,* say "It is not right of us to speak of this: glory to Thee (our LORD), this is a most serious slander!" *GOD doth admonish you, that ye may never repeat such (conduct), if ye are (true) Believers. And GOD makes the signs plain to you: for GOD is Full of Knowledge and Wisdom. Those who love (to see) scandal circulate among the Believers, will have a grievous chastisement in this life and in the hereafter: GOD knows, and ye know not. Were it not for the Grace and Mercy of GOD on you (ye would be ruined indeed) but GOD is Full of Kindness and Mercy.*"

472- [And call to thy remembrance that] it is solely GOD - *be His Magnificence celebrated!* - Who has granted thee such a fortune

473- And whenever thou spend generously in quest of His Satisfaction, He will return thee something else in place of what has been offered

474- The Advantages deriving from spending on GOD's Path (*Infāq*) and from giving charity (*Sadaqāt*) are innumerable - as admitted it all the Masters

475- It has been quoted from a <u>h</u>adīth that on the Day of Torment and Dolour, GOD, the MAJESTIC LORD, will admit some persons in Paradise

476- …Just owing to a crumb of bread, a handful of dates or whatever [largess] liable to profit to a needy person

477- By the Will of the LORD, giving charity can lead unto Paradise three kinds of persons [who played a part therein]

478-   ❶ The master of the house who gave the order to perform it,
        ❷ His wife who consented compassionately to accomplish it

479-   ❸ Their domestic who executed that action in their behalf; indeed such a grace proceeds from the MOST GENEROUS - *do ye ponder thereon!*

480- Whenever an individual gives alms, the MOST GRACIOUS will protect him from any harm,

481- From an inauspicious death, from persisting in sins and from people's grievances

482- He will also be preserved from despair, from the breaking of his kinship bonds and from a sudden and brutal death

483- The giving of a single alm can ward off seventy sorts of awful death - *retain ye that*

484- That also softens GOD's Wrath and erases our misdeeds just the way water extinguishes fire

485- On the Last Day who that has performed it will sit and rest under its "shade", while waiting for the Judgement of his fellow creatures – *so mind to hold its Advantages in high regard*

486- Charity can cure illness and, thanks to its giving, GOD pardons misdeeds - what a profitable *loan!*[39]

487- It has also been clarified that giving alms sanctifies our fortune, fends off ordeals and diseases

488- Due to its arousing lasting relief and delight in the hearts of the Believers

489- Charity enlarges our wealth, blesses it, and shields us from all the causes of downfall

490- That will make easier our Calling unto Account (*ḥisāb*) on the Day of Agony, and will make heavier [our good deeds] on the Scales

491- Charity will make smoother our Crossing of the *Sirāt* Bridge [overhanging Hell] and will raise us to lofty Degrees in Heaven

492- Charity entails GOD's Satisfaction and irritates Satan, the Cursed Outlaw

493- That allows, any such that is steadfast therein, to benefit from the prayers of the needy and of the destitute

---

[39] Cf. Qur-ān lvii. 18: "*For those who give in Charity, men and women, and loan to GOD a Beautiful Loan, it shall be increased manifold (to their credit), and they shall have (besides) a generous reward.*"

494- Charity will also increase, if sincerely fulfilled, fine afterlife Recompenses

495- However do avoid ever giving it to any such that shows blatant lack of fearing GOD

496- It is reported that some amongst the Noble Righteous were in the habit of giving everyday something

497- ...As meagre it may be, like a tiny biscuit - [because of the high significance of alms]

498- As for making discrimination in giving charity, it reported that repulsing unjustifiably a beggar in favour of another is a grave sin

499- So never forsake thy needy kin and leave afar to give showily alms [40]

500- ...As recommended by [the Prophet], the Flower of this Creation -*fasten thou on him!* -; that is to begin with ourselves, then come our closer neighbours

501- Indeed we are ordered to support first who that are directly dependent upon us, after having settled our own basic needs of course[41]

502- A Prophetic Maxim teaches [on this regard]: "*The ETERNAL-ABSOLUTE will never accept alms given in discrimination*"

---

[40]*Cf.* Qur-ān xvii. 26-27: "*And render to the kindred their due rights, as (also) to those in want, and to the wayfarer: but squander not (your wealth) in the manner of a spendthrift. Verily spendthrifts are brothers of the Satans. And the Satan is to his LORD (Himself) ungrateful.*" See also Qur-ān xvi. 90: "*GOD commands justice, the doing of good, and giving to kith and kin, and He forbids all indecent deeds, and evil and rebellion: He instructs you, that ye may receive admonition.*"
[41] "Charity beginning at home"...

503- It has also been reported from the _Hadīth_ that [the Noble Messenger has said]:_"Were it seventy thousand persons that hand over successively the same alm[42], all of them aiming thereby the Divine Satisfaction_

504- ..._The Reward imparted to the last givers will correspond to that of the first givers."_

505- The Grand Masters have stated that performing a pair of rak'a, at morning start (_Duhā_ prayer)[43], or treating impartially two persons [in conflict]

506- ...Are considered as giving alms; a word of Glorification of GOD (_Tasbīh_)[44] or of Praise to Him (_Tahmīd_)[45] are held likewise

507- So are considered any footstep taken towards the mosque or sanding up a spit on the way - _hold on to that hadīth_

508- Speaking kind and upright words to one's fellow Muslim is also regarded as giving charity by the Ancients

509- The same with sweeping voluntarily the mosque or putting on a lamp therein

510- [All of these acts are likewise considered as giving charity]: commending good, forbidding evil[46], watching over thy Brethren's honour

---

[42]X giving to Y, Y giving to Z, and so on.

[43] A traditional optional prayer of two rak'as performed within complete sunrise and noon (see verse 199).

[44]_Subhāna Lāh_: Glory to GOD!

[45]_Alhamdu li-Lāh_: Praise be to GOD!

[46]_Cf._ Qur-ān ix. 71: _"The believers, men and women, are protectors, one of another: they enjoin what is just, and forbid what is evil: they observe regular prayers, pay zakat and obey GOD and His Messenger. On them will GOD pour His mercy: for GOD is Exalted in power, Wise."_ Qur-ān iii.104: _"Let there arise out of you a band of people inviting to all that is good, enjoining what is right, and forbidding what is_

511- Sitting one's face turned towards the Ka'ba, interceding [a just cause] on someone's behalf

512- Removing a harmful item off the way, guiding a blind man that has lost his way

513- Anything thou spend of thy property [for lawful purposes], aught in thy speech that entails a Believer's happiness

514- Displaying before him smiling face, welcoming him warm-heartedly

515- Greeting him with broad smile, congratulating him in case of happy event

516- Giving him good advice liable to prompt him unto good deeds and to show him how to achieve his aims

517- [Are also held as equivalent to giving charity] helping thy Muslim Brother to answer a need insofar thou art able, living in friendly terms with him

518- Praying for him, beseeching GOD for his forgiveness, lending him money and other goods for the Face of the MAKER

519- Pouring water from thy bucket out to his receptacle is also considered to giving alms

520- Feeling sad at heart when he comes to thee seeking for some help thou art unable to fulfil

521- Providing a shoelace or an extra rope to thy Brother, helping him to get on his mount,

---

wrong: they are the ones to attain felicity." Qur-ān ii.263: *«Kind words and the covering of faults are better than charity followed by injury. »*

522- Loading his belongings upon his vehicle and other similar succours [are equivalent to giving charity]

523- Redoing thy prayer with him, even if thou hast already performed it alone before his coming

524- Quickening thy pace while going to help who that is calling for assistance

525- Lending some item to a Muslim, visiting the ill, walking in a funeral procession, taking part in the transportation of a deceased

526- Offering thy sympathy to his family, paying visit to a [virtuous] Brother, keeping company to someone that is feeling alone [are all equivalent to giving charity] - as put it [Al-Yadālī], the Headman

The Reading of the Qur-ān

and what is relating thereto

527- As for the Advantages ensuing from regular reading of the Qur-ān, they are held in great regard by the Stainless Master [Al-Yadālī]

528- *"Whoever wishes to draw nearer to his LORD, let him read the Qur-ān ceaselessly"*

529- I do add for myself: *"Whoever wishes to earn GOD's Satisfaction, let him read constantly the Qur-ān and meditate on its verses"*[47]

530- Then persist in reading the Holy Book, were it only three *hizb*[48] everyday

531- And never give up such a habit as many students commonly do nowadays

532- Some who claim to be *Sūfis* (Mystics) declare that what they are practising [as a worship] is worthier than the reading of the Qur-ān, [the reason for which they disregard it]

533- Know that such an allegation is groundless and erroneous; Satan has deluded such people - *do bring thyself closer to GOD through the Book instead*

534- Because the Sublime Qur-ān is the very basis of any true knowledge in this world - as put it the Proficient Master

---

[47]Cf. Qur-ān xxxviii. 29: *"(Here is) a Book which We have sent down unto thee, full of blessings, that they may meditate on its Signs, and that men of understanding may receive admonition "*, Qur-ān xlvii. 24: *"Do they not then earnestly seek to understand the Qur-ān, or is that there are locks upon their hearts?"* Qur-ān ii. 121: *"Those to whom We have given the Book study it as it should be studied: they are the ones that believe therein. Those who reject faith therein, the loss is their own."*
[48]Sixtieth portion of the Qur-ān.

535- Never desert it, but read thou it continually and ask for whatever sort of knowledge thou wish thereby

536- ...As did it the Virtuous Ancients; any of them has indeed quenched his thirst with the Waves of its Unfathomable Ocean

537- Do endeavour earnestly to adopt any exemplary attitude which has been praised therein by the LORD

538- And, conversely, any behaviour that has been blamed and forbidden to a creature therein, avoid it - *so wilt thou show uprightness*

539- Because the MOST HIGH LORD has just revealed it in order to be put into practice – so *do try to put its Message into practice*[49]

540- However, few verses read with meditation and understanding are preferred to the thoughtless reading of many *Surā*

541- It has been said that no one but who that meditates reflectively on its content will be rewarded thereof by the LORD of Volition

542- Nevertheless an exception has been unanimously accepted by the Masters: it concerns the student who that is learning the Qur-ān [by heart][50]; apart from this case some Doctors differ about [such a rigorous opinion][51]

543- [Regarding such a question about the importance of concentration in worship] we may quote Ibn 'Abbās - *may the LORD of Mankind be Satisfied with him, as well as with his father 'Abbās-*

---

[49]Cf. Qur-ān vi. 155: "*And this is a Book We have revealed as a blessing: so follow it and be righteous, that ye may receive mercy.*"

[50]On which case there is no divergence about his rewarding, even if he reads without meditation; this dispensation is due to the merit of such a task which is itself valuable enough...

[51] Such Doctors uphold that reading the Book is always useful, even if the reader is not really attentive...

544- Who asserts that a single pair of rak'a performed with reverence and with the heart engrossed in contemplation

545- ...Are more meritorious than praying the whole night with neglectful and heedless heart - *mind thou to be steadfast*

546/550- According to [Al-Yadālī] - the Man of the Deymān Tribe - the Rules of Reverence (*Adab*) relating to the reading of the Qur-ān are:
- Purity of body
- Cleanness of the place of reading
- Deep meditation on the meanings of the verses
- Calmness[52]
- Prior using of toothpick
- Turning in awe one's face towards the Ka'ba
- Bending one's head in veneration for GOD
- *Tafkhīm* reading, which is performed with solemn and manly voice, is preferred to effeminate voice with singsong inflections or showy rhythm [53]

551- One has also to seek through one's reading GOD's Satisfaction, out of any ostentation or material purpose

552- The reader must moreover comply with all the proprieties prescribed by his LORD and which relate to His Book

553- He must convince himself that GOD, the ABSOLUTE MASTER, is Present and is personally Speaking *to him*[54]; so he has to bear

---

[52]*Cf.* Qur-ān vii. 204-205: "*When the Qur-ān is read, listen to it with attention, and hold your peace: that ye may receive mercy. And do thou (O reader!) bring thy LORD to remembrance in thy (very) soul, with humility and remember without loudness in words, in the mornings and evenings; and be not thou of those who are unheedful.*"

[53] There are other implicit rules besides these, as the prior calling for protection against Satan ('*Adhbala*), the saying of the *Basmalah* and so. *Cf.* Qur-ān xvi. 98: "*When thou dost read the Qur-ān, seek GOD's protection from Satan the Rejected One.*"

constantly in mind that the words he is reading originates undoubtedly from his Very LORD

554- The servant must read the Qur-ãn as if he was *actually* watching the LORD - *may He be Glorified! (Indeed on naught will we ever rely but Him)*

555- Because [as quoted from the Qur-ãn[55]] even if no eye can grasp Him, as for Him, HE is watching on all His creatures

556- [Now, regarding times appointed for the reading of the Qur-ãn], there is actually no prohibited time for such a reading - according to the Reliable Masters

557- As for those who blame it within the Late Afternoon Prayer (*'Aṣr*) and the Sunset Prayer (*Maghrib*), we must not take into account their banning

558- Furthermore we have to refute their trifling reasoning: Jews are used to do their studies on that time [the reason why Muslims have to refrain from doing the same]

559- The best time to read the Qur-ãn comes during nocturnal prayers, mostly that performed in the last part of the night

560- ...Or within the Sunset Prayer (*Maghrib*) or the Night Prayer (*'Ishã*); reading the Book after performance of the Morning Prayer (*Subḥ*) is also exalted by the highly Skilled Master

---

[54]*Cf*. Qur-ãn ii. 186: "*When My servants ask thee concerning Me, I am indeed close (to them): I respond to the prayer of every suppliant when he calleth on Me: let them also, with a will, listen to My call, and believe in Me, that they may walk in the right way.*"

[55]*Cf*. Qur-ãn vi. 103:"*No vision can grasp Him, but His grasp is over all vision; He is Subtle, Well-Aware*" and iii. 163:"*...And GOD sees well all that they do.*"

561- [As for its favourite days], know that Monday, Thursday and Friday [out of any week], and the day of *Arafāt* [the 9th day of the yearly Pilgrimage] are well esteemed

562- Reading the Qur-ān from a book (*Mushaf*) plainly laid before one's eyes is preferable to its reciting by heart

563- For whenever thou read from the Book, for the Holy Face of GOD,

564- ...Thou wilt relieved thy parents of some afterlife hardships, by the Leave of the MAJESTIC LORD

565- Whosoever runs often his eyes over the Holy Book will also be granted good eyesight by the LORD of humankind

566- And his parents' chastisement in the grave[56] will be lightened, were they giving partners to GOD (*Mushrikūn*)

567- Twelve out of the Noble Companions of the Prophet have unanimously asserted that such a way of reading the Qur-ān is more meritorious than accomplishing many other sorts of good deeds

568- Some Masters, construing this, say that such a pre-eminence is due to that reading from a tangible book keeps busy as well our tongues as our eyes

569- Such a way of reading is also [more liable] to monopolise the heart, the hands[57], the legs[58] and so the mind[59]

570- However if thou feel more concentrated and if thou meditate better in reciting the Qur-ān by heart

---

[56]If the case arises of course.
[57]Hands: holding and leafing through the *Mushaf.*
[58]Legs: tucked in a sitting posture.
[59] Mind: not diverted from meditation by any sense.

571- …Rather than in reading from a *Mushaf*, it is preferable for thee to recite it by heart

572- Staying a whole day without glancing at the Qur-ān is considered as blameful by the August Masters

573- Because, according to them, a single glance cast over the Book is counted as an act of worship

574- There is however a divergence as to know which mode of recitation is better:
- *Tartīl* reading (uttering softly and clearly)
- Or fast reciting
Each side has put forward well-founded arguments

575- The main argument of *tartīl*-side reading consists in this Koranic Recommendation: "*...and recite the Qur-ān in slow, measured rhythmic tones (tartīl)* " (lxxiv. 4)

576- Their opponents have also taken their evidence from the Book: "*[O ye who believe!] mention GOD abundantly*" (xxxiii. 41)

577- [Just content thyself in knowing that whatever mode one might adopt], the basic principle and objective of such Heavenly Injunctions remains meditating and understanding the Koranic Message - yea!

578- All of the Masters agreed that both modes of reciting are conform to the Prophetic Tradition (*Sunna*) - never then denigrate one of them

579- [An evidence of the importance of the Qur-ān is this Maxim of the Best Creature]: "*The best among you is he who learned the Qur-ān and then taught it*"

580- Knowing by heart the Qur-ān is a Community Obligation (*Fard Kifāya*) - as conveyed to us-

581- If there are enough members of the Muslim Community who know it by heart so as to ensure its right conveyance [to the next generation, others will be released from such a duty]

582- But in case that quorum of teachers is not reached then all the Community will be at fault

583- Teaching the Qur-ãn [is most valuable], were it in return for wages, because this has been judged lawful by the Imam Mãlik

584- ...Basing on the Holy Prophet's words - *may Peace and Blessings be bestowed upon him, upon his Family, his Companions and all that are following in his footsteps -*

585- *"The best work for which ye can receive wages is the teaching of GOD's Book"*

586- [Such a remuneration has been legitimated] for fear of losing GOD's Word due to lack of reading and of right conveyance

587- Kissing the *Mushaf*, as one would do with his beloved little child, is also held as estimable

588- The same with putting it on a desk and perfuming it, out of respect - o Dear Brother!

589- But it is positively forbidden to lay one's head on it by way of a pillow; this is quite unlawful

590- The same with putting something on it, like other books, pieces of wood and other weighty items

591- It is not convenient to stretch out one's legs towards the Holy Book or to carry it everywhere with oneself - *do avoid all of this*

592- It is advisable to transcribe its Vulgate in attractive and legible handwriting

593- ...With accurate presentation and flawless correctness devoid of any clerical error or other mistakes; hence an excessively reduced writing is considered as blameful

594- Or the use of small sheets of paper to make therewith a tiny *Mus̲h̲af*

595- [Note that] the vocalisation of the Qur-ãn and its marks of punctuation have been appended afterwards[60] so as to safeguard the Book from later wrong meanings

596- An account taken from the Imam Mãlik considers as blameful dividing up the Book into small portions (*juz*)[61]

597- ...Basing on GOD's Sublime Word - *Glory to Him!* -: **"It is for Us to collect it and to recite it."** (Lxxv. 17)

598- Enumerating all that is relating to the Revealed Book would lead us too far indeed

599- Let us get back now to the core of this piece of poetry - *may we be assisted on such a task by the LORD of Volition*

600- [All the more so since] the enlightenments above should suffice [as an incitement to seek for] the Benefits [deriving from the reading of the Qur-ãn]. Let us now take up the subject of Sufism

---

[60] During the caliphate of U̲t̲h̲mãn (the 3rd Caliph of Islam).
[61] Thirtieth portion of the Qur-ãn.

Sufism

(At-Tasawwuf)

601- According to our Eminent Imam Al-Ghazāli:*"Keeping pure one's heart and worshipping the LORD in accordance with the Rules of Sufism is an individual obligation (Farḏ 'Ayn) for any Muslim"*

602/603- We may mention here seven main Pillars of such a way of life:

❶ Keeping often silent [out of any vain chattering]
❷ Withstanding hunger
❸ Departing from any falsity
❹ Genuine repentance
❺ Night worship
❻ Keeping often aloof from people
❼ Perfect uprightness - *what marvellous virtues!*

604- To these seven qualities, our dear Sheikh Al-Yadālī added an eight one that is:

❽ Fearing inwardly and outwardly GOD

605- As regards withdrawing from people [the 6th point], it becomes compulsory if man has a definite ground to fear for the perversion of his faith in frequenting society[62]

606- Or when people are plunged into deep confusion and moral disorder one is not capable of resolving - otherwise cutting oneself from one's fellow creatures is forbidden

---

[62]Withdrawing completely from society is forbidden in Islam, the reason why Christian monasticism is condemned in the Qur-ān (lvii. 27): *"But the Monasticism which they invented for themselves, We did not prescribe for them: (We commanded) only the seeking for the Good Pleasure of GOD."* One may also quote in this regard this Prophetic *hadith* (though commonly controversial): *"Lã rahbāniyya fi-l-Islãm"* (No Monasticism in Islam!)

607- [It has been however wondered if], outside the two cases above-mentioned, it would not be more profitable to a servant to mingle with people so as to benefit from the manifold advantages one may obtain [through services one can do to people]

608- ...Or if it would not be preferable, for any spiritual beginner (al-Murīd), to stay by himself so as to guard himself from ostentation and to benefit from the unremitting acts of worship [privacy allows to perform]

609- Indeed this last alternative may be better if solitude leads us unto profitable meditation and if we cannot bear patiently harm stemming from mixing with people

610- ...And if furthermore we are not behaving so out of pride and if our help for social affairs is not required - *surely!*

611- But supposing that one succeeds in perfectly withstanding society drawbacks or supposing that solitude entails for us no useful meditation and contemplation [of GOD's Grandeur]

612- ...Or if one keeps aloof just out of disdain [for *the common herd*] or in fearing selfishly to face social problems,

613- ...It would be then more advisable to take the habit of mingling with people - if, once again, one is able to steer clear of society vices - *know thou that*

614- In case our assistance is called on to fulfil some social need or to put right a troublesome situation, joining people becomes then mandatory

615- And as long as that problem will remain unsolved [we will be compelled to stay at the Community's disposal]; we will, for instance, go on teaching people, attending congregational prayers and so

616- As for the definition of True Repentance [the 4th Pillar of Taṣawwuf], that is: giving up sinning, remorsefully and without delay, in Awe of the LORD

617- However such a stopping of sinning must be done deliberately, but not against one's will; as a dumb person [prevented from scandalmongering by his disability] or [a debauchee prevented from fornicating] by some venereal disease and so forth[63]

618- Nay! But one has to withdraw from sinning in the sole order to magnify GOD, the INCOMMENSURABLE, and for fear of His Grievous Chastisement

619- ...With keen remorse for having lapsed into sins and vices in the past

620- ...And with sincere intention to never relapse into aught that would displease the ETERNAL-ABSOLUTE LORD in the future

621- [Another condition of genuine Repentance is] making up for material and moral damages we caused in the past to their rightful claimants - as I once said it in certain verses

622- Refer to one of our book based on an Al-Akhdarī's work[64], ye will find therein other clarifications [on the conditions of true Repentance] as bright as moonlight

---

[63]"...the same with a blind man [prevented from looking at indecencies] or a deaf person [prevented from listening to unlawful speech]..."
[64]Jawhāru-n-Nafīs (The Precious Jewel), a book of Islamic Law about the rules of worship, composed by the Sheikh about 1294 H. (1876/77), at the age of about 25 (Cf. the work Irwāu-n-Nadīm (The Quenching of the Table Companion) of Muḥammad-al-Amīn DIOP, one of the fortunate witness and the biographer of the Sheikh's life). The verses in reference are 13 to 29: " [The responsible individual (mukallaf)] has to do his utmost to perform Heavenly Prescriptions and to avoid Godly Proscriptions; he must also devote himself to genuine repentance, examining everyday his conscience for the Countenance of his LORD - may His Glory be celebrated! - before His Wrath fall on him... Amongst the

623- People of this generation - I tell you - disregard *Tasawwuf* practice; much good they are losing indeed!

624- Because they ignore that *Tasawwuf* is the Kingly Way towards GOD's Neighbourhood (*Hadratu-l-Lāh*): soon will they fade away

625- They know not that the practising of *Tasawwuf* is the Best Provision [man can hold in store] for the Day of Great Loss and Fright

626- They know not that the Science of Heart Purification is the best Knowledge on which man can spend his whole lifetime

---

clauses of such repentance, one may count (1) deep regrets for past sins, whatever these may be, (2) sincere resolution to never relapse, for the rest of one's life, into [similar faults] that would be detrimental [to one's salvation] and (3) refraining forthwith from further sins, if presently transgressing. But neither must he retard his repentance nor postpone it, nor is he entitled to say: "I will wait until [GOD] that has Might of Forgiveness, lead me on the straight path..."; *for that is verily a sign of abandonment [by GOD]* (khidhlān), *a sign of damnation and of tarnished heart - I seek my LORD's Protection from these two misfortunes... The compensation to the victims for all the injustices committed in the past is likewise included amongst the clauses of true repentance, according to who that is obedient (Al Akhdarī), because this is a Divine Obligation and, thenceforth, whosoever fails to fulfil it out of heedlessness has disobeyed his MASTER. Now as regarding injustices, they may be divided into two sorts: (1) damage to property and (2) moral damage. Thus the penitent has to redress his damages to others' property in favour of the rightful claimants if these can be found - out of any spirit of unfairness. In case they cannot be found, he must make due amends to their heirs with no hesitation; but for lack of finding the heirs, he should give equivalent alms on their behalf; so reported it who that is veracious (Al Akhdarī)... The repentant has also to unburden himself off the moral damages caused to others through, for instance, scandalmongering, offences or glaring slander, [by apologising to the injured person] if this one is present; otherwise, if this last cannot be met again, the penitent have to increase his pious deeds so as to gain enough deeds of worship liable [on the Day of Reckoning] to atone for the infringed rights of those moral victims and, in so doing, the* mukallaf *should ask for remission of his wrong deeds, hoping for his LORD's Oft-forgiveness..."*

627- They ignore that *Tasawwuf* leads unto Uprightness and takes away from the Divine Blame

628- Some of them, whose hearts are filled with disease[65] and hatred, have even come to condemn its practising!

629- Some others, applying thereto the term of "extremism", hold it as a groundless exaggeration of worship

630- Some amongst them criticise *Tasawwuf* practice just because of laziness, immoderate love for earthly pleasures and out of cowardice

631- Some others, deluded by their heedlessness, say: "*This is obviously fanaticism!*"

632- Certain people, quite convinced of its unlawfulness, have decided to turn definitely a deaf ear to the Call of *Tasawwuf*, as if there were some seals cast in their ears

633- Some never cease from letting fly scathing diatribes [towards Mystics] and from disparaging books which are consecrated thereto

634- [Woe to them!] Because their total ignorance about the guidance provided by *Tasawwuf* and about the obvious Benefits it entails [will never alter the Eternal Truth]

635- "*The sun would not be really_hazy just owing to a blind man that is unable to discern it overhead*"

636- "*The fog before a short-sighted person cannot hide really_the full moonlight*"

---

[65]The word *marad* is often found in the Book and concern mainly the hypocrites. *Cf.* Qur-ān ii. 10:"*In their hearts is a disease; and GOD has increased their disease: and grievous is the chastisement they (incur), because they lied to themselves*"

637- *"A High Way will not be deserted just because of a trifling ant that consents not to walk therein"*

638- Nay! He that is pure will never be *sulliIed* by the libellous remarks uttered by a *sullied* individual that exclaims, *"**He is not pure!**"*

639- The Great Masters' loftiness will not be lowered in the slightest by the envy of some experienced persons or the ignorance of some silly men

640- What an incredible behaviour! How can one disparage such knowledge which leads the servant unto a Priceless Treasure!

641- How can a sensible person come to treat scornfully such knowledge one acquires through disregarding worldly goods and which lifts man towards Eternal Bliss!?

642- What! How can we denigrate an Authentic Knowledge which comprehends all the Advantages imparted to the Men of Merit?

643- ...A kind of Wisdom which has originated as well the Fine Qualities of the Prophets as the Saints' Uprightness and the kindness of many virtuous creatures?

644- Whoever keeps on disparaging *Taṣawwuf* all the time, without repenting

645- ...Will irremediably perish, plunged into deadly sins by Divine Justice

646- ...Without even him grasping the true significance of his mistake - our Eminent Sheikh has given thereon explicit particulars - *wilt thou not awaken?*

647- For further clarifications we may refer to the book "The Shield of the GOD-seeker " (*Junnatu-l-Murīd*) composed by our Saviour, the Upright Caliph [Sīdi Mukhtār Kuntiyu]

648- *May GOD, the MAKER, be Satisfied with him as with any other kindly person amongst the Elect*

649- Now, concerning the etymology of the word *"Tasawwuf "*, differing theses have been put forward here and there

650- Some suggest the terms *"Sũfah"*, others *"Saff"*, some others *"Sũf"* or *"Safw"*[66]

651- Manifold other propositions have been suggested thereon; each of them being supported by plausible arguments

652- However such hypotheses, exceeding one thousand, appear to us irrelevant to be all enumerated here

653- [Just know that] the true *Sũfi*[67] is an erudite person who puts rigorously his knowledge into practice, out of any sin

654- ...So as to become free of any impurity and to have his heart filled with deep and wise thoughts

655- Turning his back [on worldly advantages arising from] his fellow creatures and making resolutely his way towards his CREATOR, he holds as equals gold coin and clod of earth

656- He resembles [by his forbearance] to the ground on which any sorts of refuse are thrown but which produces in return only good things

---

[66] The etymology of the word *"Tasawwuf "* arose manifold differing hypothesises, the most commonly accredited of them being (1) *"Sũf"*: woollen rustic clothes the first Mystics were in the habit of wearing; (2) *"Saff"*: rank, because the *Sũfis* stand at the first rank before GOD; (3) *"Sũfah"*: pew, because the *Sũfis* live as did the first Companions of the Prophet (PBH), called "the People of the Pew"; (4) *"Safw"*: the Elite.
[67] *Sũfi:* who that practises truly *Tasawwuf.*

657- A noble heart as well as a villain, a virtuous man as well as a sinner will trample it underfoot whereas it remains always impassive

658- The True _Ṣūfi_ is like cloud whose shadow extends over every house or like rain that pours indiscriminately its showers over the lands

659- Any that has reached such a stage [of detachment] is undeniably a real _Ṣūfi_, but as for he who has not attained such a degree and who claims to be a _Ṣūfi_, he is a real impostor!

660- Here will come to an end the preamble of this work, let us now get on to its first chapter[68]

Mosque of Touba

---

[68] Note the significance of the number of verses of the preamble (660) which is a multiple of 66: the numerical value of the word "GOD" in accordance with the calculation system used by Mystics ("GOD" is composed by four arabic letters whose respective numerical values are: "_Alīf_"(1) + "_Lām_" (30) + "_Lām_" (30) + "_Ha_"(5) = 66). In this same instance, one may also guess that the number of the verses of this last part devoted to _Taṣawwuf_ (60) and that of the preceding part (600) are not at all gratuitous...

CHAPTER 1

The Creatures

661- Do know - *may GOD preserve us from any source of peril and lead us all unto the Best Path -*

662- ...That turning to the creatures [and relying on their help] sets a barrier between the servant and [GOD], the Only Truth

663- Among the creatures one must count as well Lust and Satan, the Cursed One - *do thwart both of them, so wilt thou remain upright*

LUST
(HAWÃ)

664- Thy Lust has to be kept tightly under the control of thy reason; never let the reverse happen because that would bring to thee GOD's Wrath

665- A true believer is who that makes his way towards the LORD [guided by his reason] not by his Lust[69]

666- Bliss to he that is led towards his MASTER's Satisfaction by his intelligence, not by his passions

SATAN

667- As for [Satan], the Outcast - *we seek refuge in the MERCIFUL against him and against any blameful transgressor -*

668- ...He is an implacable and indomitable brawler who assaults man ceaselessly and never consents to settle a "peace covenant"

---

[69]Cf. Qur-ãn xxv. 43-44: "*Seest thou such a one as taketh for his god his own passion (or impulse)? Couldst thou be a disposer of affairs for him? Or thinkest thou that most of them listen or understand? They are only like cattle; - nay, they are farther astray from the way.*"

669- And whenever thou throw him down on the ground, he swiftly gets back on his feet and heads again for thee, more resolved and more dangerous than ever

670- He has committed himself to combating any servant of GOD, with no volte-face

671- [His first attack consists in] inciting the worshipper to give up adoring; if the servant resists [in persevering bravely in acting], he will induce him unto performing expeditiously his pious deeds so as to spoil them

672- If the servant still persists in not submitting, *Iblīs*[70] will urge him unto displaying showily his good deeds in order to be admired by people; if man still escapes such a danger and strives unto concealing his actions

673- ...The Stoned One will attempt to fill his heart with self-conceit and to make him behave haughtily vis-à-vis his fellow servants[71] and so forth - until the servant succumbs to his assaults

674- [O my Brother!] do keep a watchful eye on Satan and always be ready to repel him and to defend gallantly thyself - *so wilt thou be rid of trouble-*

675- When he inspires thee with evil suggestions repel him by the "Sword" of *Dhikr*[72], so wilt thou win Saintliness

676- Do seek Protection against him from thy LORD, the BOUNTIFUL, Who will shield thee from his Mighty Snare[73]

---

[70] Satan's Koranic name.

[71] Others who have not, as him, succeed in stepping over Satan's fiendish traps...

[72] Remembrance and utterance of GOD's Names (*Cf.* verses 299-408). We may read in the Holy Book: *"Those who fear GOD, when a thought of evil from Satan assaults them, bring GOD to remembrance, when lo! They see (aright)!"* (Qur-ān vii. 201)

677- For - [never forget it] - Satan is naught but a *dog* urged onto thee by the LORD Then do call for his *MASTER* 's Help and delude not thyself![74]

678- For if ever thou undertake to battle unaided against him, without asking beforehand GOD's Assistance, thou wilt soon realise thy impotence

679- If thou underrate him, he will injure thee seriously and if thou commit the mistake to fight alone, no doubt he will slaughter thee!

680- Let us call to remembrance his famous story with the named Birsīs[75]

---

[73]*Cf.* Qur-ān xvi.99-100: "*No authority has [Satan] over those who believe and put their trust in their LORD. His authority is over those only, who take him as patron and who join partners with GOD.*" Qur-ān vii. 27: " *O ye Children of Adam! Let not Satan seduce you, in the same manner as he got your parents out of the Garden, stripping them on their raiment, to expose their shame: for he and his tribe see you from a position where ye cannot see them: We made the Satans friends (only) to those without faith.*" Qur-ān xvii. 63-64: "*(GOD) said:* "Go thy way [O Iblīs!]; if any of them follow thee, verily Hell will be the recompense of you (all)- an ample recompense. And arouse those whom thou canst among them with thy (seductive) voice; make assaults on them with thy cavalry and thy infantry; mutually share with them wealth and children; and make promises to them." *But Satan promises them nothing but deceit.* "As for My Servants, no authority shalt thou have over them": *enough is thy LORD for a DISPOSER of affairs.*" Qur-ān vii. 200: "*If a suggestion from Satan assail thy (mind), seek refuge with GOD; for He heareth and knoweth (all things).*"
[74]Indeed as paradoxical as it may appear at first sight, Satan's power proceeds from GOD's. *Cf.* Qur-ān xxxviii. 82-83: "*(Iblis) said:*" Then by **Thy power**, *I will lead them all astray. Except Thy Servants amongst them, sincere and purified (by Thy grace)*"" This paradox is mainly grounded by the necessity of "evil" and "danger" on earth so as to urge man to commit himself to GOD and to prefer future Life…
[75] Birsīs is said to be an hermit who left social life and retired in the wilderness to adore better his LORD. When some girl fell seriously ill, Satan inspired her parents that only Birsīs could cure her. Despite of his reluctance

681- Or his story with Bal'ãm who was yet an Ocean of knowledge[76] - indeed such stories should be sufficient as a piece of admonition

682- Then never feel safe and definitely secure from Satan's pitfalls until the very day when thy soul will split off thy body for good

683- Because [it has been said that] he may appear [in a luring form] to a dying Muslim and try to deprive him of the fruits of his good deeds [with deceitful promises]

684- As yself, I do take shelter under my LORD's Safeguard whenever he assaults me[77]

---

he was finally compelled to take her in for some time. So was he led to succumb to temptation and to lapse from Divine Grace.

[76]Bal'ãm son of Beor was a seer living in the times of the Prophet Moses - Peace and Blessings upon him-. It is said that he was called out by the king of Moab, Balak, - who provided him with plenty gifts- to curse the Children of Israel, his enemies. After some hesitation he agreed to anathematise Israel but an Angel appeared to him and he was compelled to bless them instead! Some commentators think that these Koranic verses (vii. 175-176) refer to his story: *"Relate to them the story of the man to whom We sent Our Signs, but he passed them by: so Satan followed him up, and he went astray. If it had been Our Will, We should have elevated him with Our Signs: but he inclined to the earth, and followed his own vain desires"*

[77] The effectiveness of such an attitude of total surrender and reliance in GOD's Protection was later demonstrated by the very existence of the Sheikh himself and by formal assertions he happened to write after the famous episode of Jèwol (a Senegalese locality where Sheikh Aḥmadu Bamba met the French official emissary on August 10th, 1895. *Cf.* also Tome IV, Appendix A): *"In Jèwol, GOD has put Satan in despair of ever harming me as I was striving to implore Him:* "O Thou my PROTECTOR!" (*Cf.* the poem "Ayãsa..." composed as an acrostic of the verse *"As for My Servants, no authority shalt thou have over them"*(xvii. 64)) Moreover, in one of his last books Sheikh Aḥmadu Bamba wrote: *"I have parted for good with Satan and with any seed of debasement and - by the Holy Name of GOD, the MOST GRACIOUS, the MOST MERCIFUL - I have fastened up with GOD's Messenger (May GOD grant him Peace and Blessings) and with all the beneficial deeds... Thanks to the Qur-ãn I live eternally with my LORD, the Matchless ASSISTANT; I*

The Basic Drives
(Nafs)

685- Thy *Nafs* (basic drives) belongs also to the creatures; do watch on her because she is man's most harmful enemy - as conveyed by the Prophetic Tradition

686- Never give in to her whims or satisfy her wishes, o Dear Fellow! Be thou harsh and austere with her instead

687- Because man's honour and tribute [in the Hereafter] will depend on the number of aversions he overcame and on the hardness of the troubles he made his *Nafs* undergo [in life here below]

688- Do struggle with her in accomplishing [in "rain or shine"] GOD's Command so as to uphold His Word above all, o thou that art shrewd!

689- Call her continuously to account so as to make easier thy *Hisāb* (Calling to Account) before the ETERNAL-ABSOLUTE on the Last Day

690- Remind her all the time death and the Formidable Dread following on it; let not her lead thee unto dissipating thy lifetime

691- Stay always watchful and on thy guard against her just as one would do if he meets a lion in the bush who is getting ready to leap over him

---

have perfectly mastered my soul and have driven away Satan, the Damned. Of this world I just content myself with drawing therefrom my provisions for Paradise; I have entirely mastered my lust and have purified my heart " (Cf. "Jāwartu bi-l-Furqān...")

692- There is no doubt that such a person would be afraid [and would stand extremely cautious!] because the slightest while of heedlessness would put him at the mercy of the wildcat

693- Nonetheless one can realise [on second thoughts] that such a situation is in fact a *benefit* from GOD

694- Because confronting with such a fierce enemy [as the *Nafs*] should incite man unto appealing to GOD's Help, if naturally that person leans to cleansing his soul so as to lift it towards the LORD

This Present World

(Dunyā)

695- Amongst the creatures is this vile world which is regarded as worthless and highly negligible by GOD - *to Whom belongs True Religion* - [78]

696- Turn thy heart aside from it in practising asceticism (*Zuhd*) so as to be secured from the luring temptations it displays

697- True asceticism is just ceasing from aiming in one's heart worldly purpose for GOD's Holy Face

698- So neither be overjoyed by the obtaining of earthly goods nor be saddened by material deprivation

---

[78]About this valueless world the Holy Book teaches us: "*Know ye (all), that the life of this world is but play and a pastime, adornment and mutual boasting and multiplying, (in rivalry) among yourselves, riches and children. Here is a similitude: how rain and the growth which it brings forth, delight (the hearts of) the tillers; soon it withers, thou wilt see it grow yellow; then it becomes dry and crumbles away. But in the Hereafter is a Chastisement severe (for the devotees of wrong). And Forgiveness from GOD and (His) Good Pleasure (for the devotees of GOD). And what is the life of this world, but goods and chattels of deception?*" (Qur-ān lvii. 20); "*As to these, they love the fleeting life, and put away behind them a Day (that will be) hard.*" (Qur-ān lxxvi. 27); "*The mutual rivalry for piling up (the good things of this world) diverts you (from the more serious things), until ye visit the graves. But nay, ye soon shall know (the reality). Again, ye soon shall know! Nay, were ye to know with certainly of mind, (ye would beware!). Ye shall certainly see Hell-fire! Again, ye shall see it with certainty of sight! Then, shall ye be questioned that Day about the joy (ye indulged in!)*" (Qur-ān Sūrah cii) "*Those who rest not their hope on their meeting with Us, but are pleased and satisfied with the life of the Present, and those who heed not Our signs, - their abode is the Fire because of the (evil) they earned.*" (Qur-ān x. 7)

699- Because loving this present world is, of surety, the chief root of any peril but [unfortunately] this reality eludes often people

700- All evils originate from concupiscence, the reason for which any sensible and self-restrained person will disregard earthly affairs

701/703- [Regarding worldly things, they can be divided into three sorts]
❶ Unlawful things, which entail eviction [from the Sphere of Divine Mercy], chastisement, extreme spiritual destitution and veiling

❷ Things whose lawfulness is doubtful; their use will lead toward Divine Reprimand, darkness, quarrel and blame on the Resurrection Day

❸ Lawful things whose use in arrogance will induce however tough Calling unto Account (Hisāb); as for making use of them just for rivalry and for vain competition, that will bring about punishment on Doomsday

704- Indeed any who uses [licit goods] just for pleasure and sport will be subject to questioning and detention in the Hereafter[79] - *never doubt ye about*

705- However keeping lawful goods as a precautionary measure or seeking for them just out of compassion for one's fellow creatures or in the view to support oneself

706- ...So as to be able to manage without people and, thus, to safeguard one's faith and honour, [such noble motives] entitle to gain the finest reward

---

[79]Cf. Qur-ān ii. 168: "*O ye people! Eat of what is on earth, lawful and good; and do not follow the footsteps of Satan for he is to you an avowed enemy.*"

707- Know that having at one's disposal the bare essentials in this world is better than poverty and better than wealth kept to prepare for hard times

708- A wealthy person who shows true gratefulness to GOD is considered as superior to a poor person who shows patience[80]

709- When consuming worldly goods, be as temperate as who that is compelled to eat a carcass out of necessity

710- [Just live in this world] as a foreigner in exile who is imprisoned therein [and who is musing with nostalgia over the wonders of his paradisiacal "native country"]; then do endure stoically worldly adversities and hardships [81]

711- Because the misfortunes of this world - like poverty, diseases and other unexpected ordeals

712- ...Such as disasters, calamities, hunger, painful situations and damages

713- All of that are in fact a *good* proceeding from [GOD] Who that holds Majesty – so explained it Al-Yadālī:

714- *"Any that is entirely exempt from Divine trials will undoubtedly enjoy staying in this world and so he will hold it as an eternal paradise in which he would dwell blissfully forever*

---

[80] Because beign compelled to bear patience by necessity is easier than remembring the LORD in times of happiness, to some extents...

[81] In waiting for your "Liberation Day" *i.e.* the day when you will enter Heaven... This is conform to the Hadith *"Dunyā sijnu-l-mūminīn wa jannatu-l-Kāfir"* (This world is a prison for the Believers and a paradise for the unbelievers)

715- *Such a one will be eventually averse to meeting GOD and will come to loathe death, in so doing, wishing inconsequently to stay immortal! "*

716- Worldly misfortunes have also the merit to incite man unto turning towards our MAJESTIC LORD for alleviation and to treat despisingly life here below

717- Indeed the best state of mind for a believing servant is constantly humbling himself and feeling clearly the necessity to appeal to the ETERNAL-ABSOLUTE

718- Because [facing insoluble problems] may lead him to realise that there are no means or absolute appearances one may rely on outside the MOST GRACIOUS, the ONLY ONE

719- ...[In Whose sole Help the servant must confide[82]] as a solitary wayfarer lost in the desert or an isolated swimmer drowning deep into the water

720- The worst state of mind for a human is confiding entirely in one's ability or esteeming too much the power of any creature

721- Or leaning on someone else, were it for his knowledge, his qualities or his outstanding deeds

722- Indeed the feeling of humbleness deriving from sinning or from undergoing firmly a trial is more meritorious than exhilarating feeling of grandeur ensuing from one's uprightness or from one's gifts

723-Because, in the first case, man is led to be aware of his own weakness and inadequacy; he also becomes afraid of sinning again and so he will redeem himself

---

[82]*Cf.* Qur-ān lxvii. 29: "*Say:*" He is the MOST GRACIOUS: we have believed in Him, and on Him have we put our trust""

724- [Erring or suffering may also] prompt the soul to turning definitely towards the Next World and to aspiring after the Divine Reward, if of course man consents to amend rapidly

725- It may urge the servant to returning to GOD, to worshipping in discretion and pure-heartedness, to GOD's Remembrance and this may cure his vices

726- O Dear Friend! Know that a good deed performed secretely is worthier than a good deed performed publicly - *this is unanimously agreed on*

727- Because such a concealment is harder to bear for the Soul, due to its depriving her of people's praising

People

728- Our fellow humans belong likewise to the creatures: never entrust thy hopes to them, o my Companion! And act not out of fear of them - *so wilt thou be honoured*

729- Never complain before the *creatures* about thy needs but do appeal to their Very *CREATOR*, the WILLPOWERED LORD

730- [Turn thy will towards Him] and never towards them - be they behaving favourably with thee or not - and call GOD's Infinite Knowledge to witness [of thy acts]

731/734-
Always look at them with two kinds of eyes:
❶ With the eyes of *Shari'a*[83], in commending them good, in forbidding them all kinds of evil, in sanctioning them if necessary and in thanking them for their kindnesses

---

[83] Islamic Law which deals with human acts (*Cf.* verses 80-82)

❷ With the eyes of *Haqīqah*[84], in forgiving their faults, in never bearing them a grudge for their injustices or when thou art refused a service or even if they hurt thee

735- Because they are all ruled by the Absolute Decree of the MOST GRACIOUS and are constantly governed by His Command

736- Thence it is ultimately thy LORD MOST HIGH Who prevented thee from obtaining thy wish and Who caused what harmed thee, nay the creatures!

737- So never hurt them, do acknowledge their rights and bear patiently their grievances[85]

738- Be at any time ready to help them and to express thy affection and thy mercy to them out of any sort of envy

739- Show them virtuous and fine qualities *outwardly* while revering only the LORD *in thy inmost heart* – do combine both of these, [so wilt thou reunite *Shari'a* and *Haqīqah*]

740- Behave towards thy fellow creatures with solicitude, compassion and pure-heartedness, wish them good and safety

741- Do resort to thy LORD against their injustices, o my Friend! So wilt thou realise that such injustices are in fact *Godsends!*[86]

---

[84] In Islam, knowledge of deeper realities that deals with spiritual states and other transcendental considerations.

[85] Such an *elevation d'âme* is recommended by the Qur-ān: "*And if ye punish, let your punishment be proportionate to the wrong that has been done to you. But if ye show patience, that is indeed the best (course) for those who are patient.*" (xvi.126)

[86] Since such injustices drove you eventually to resort to the LORD! Cf. Qur-ān vii. 94-95: "*Whenever We sent a prophet to a town, We took up its people in suffering and adversity,* **in order that they might call in humility.** *Then We changed their suffering into prosperity, until they grew and multiplied, and began to say:* "Our fathers (too) were touched by suffering and affluence". *Behold! We took them to account of a sudden, while they realised not (their peril).* "

Human Deeds

742- Our deeds are also counted among the creatures: so never rely on them whatever they may be

743- Be not too confident in them, expecting thereby future rewarding and favours because of the likely minute imperfections [liable to spoil them] which will appear on the Day of <u>H</u>isāb (Calling to Account)

744- Because also, as considerable as they may be, they are not really thine; [thou hast not truly performed them][87]- *let not thyself be deluded by [Satan], the Master of Snares*

745/746- Purify them in acting sincerely and, even if one day thou art let in the House of Truth [the "Paradise of thy good deed"], content thyself in saying: *"Aught my LORD wills happens and, verily, there is no means or power but in GOD, the MOST HIGH!"*

---

[87]Indeed a deeper knowledge shows that man's good deeds originate from GOD's Will. *Cf.* Qur-ān iv. 78-79: " *If some good befalls them they [the Hypocrites] say, 'This is from GOD'; but if evil, they say, 'This is from thee [O Prophet]'. Say: 'All things are from GOD. " But what hath come to these people that they fail to understand a single fact? Whatever good, (O man!), happens to thee, is from GOD; but whatever evil happens to thee, is from thyself (...) "* Here is the commentary of these verses in Yusuf Ali's translation of the Qur-ān (p. 236, note 597): " *The Hypocrites were inconsistent, and this reflects unregenerate mankind. If a disaster happens, due to their own folly, they blame somebody else; but if they are fortunate, they claim reflected credit by pretending that Heaven has favoured them because of their own superior merits. The modern critic discards even this pretence, eliminates Heaven altogether, and claim all credit direct to himself, unless he brings in blind Chance, but that he does mostly to " explain " misfortune. If we look to the ultimate Cause of all things, all things come from GOD. But if we look to the proximate cause of things, our own merit is so small, that we can hardly claim credit for good ourselves with any fairness. In GOD's hand is all good: iii.26. On the other hand, the proximate cause of evil is due to some wrong in our own inner selves; for never are we dealt with unjustly in the very least: iv.77.*"

Complements

about deeds and dangerous delusions

747- The Beacon of Religion, our learned Sheikh Ibn 'Atã' Lãh, has said in the beginning of his book called *Al-Hikam* (Pieces of Wisdom)

748- *"The fact that man's hope [in the future reward] lessens if he commits an offence is the evidence that he leans naturally on his acts"*

749- I do add, as myself, that: " *Is likewise a sign of man's natural reliance on his deeds his being quite convinced of his salvation because of his asceticism, his self-restraint and his acts of worship"*[88]

---

[88] *Cf.* Qur-ãn xxiv. 21: " *Were it not for the grace and mercy of GOD on you, not one of you would ever have been pure: but GOD doth purify whom He pleases and GOD is One who hears and knows (all things)."* *Cf.* also Qur-ãn iii. 188: *"Think not those who exult in what they have brought about, and who love to be praised for what they have not done, - think not that they can escape the Chastisement. For them is a Chastisement grievous indeed."* Commenting this last verse, the Eminent Emir Abd-el-Kader (1808-1883, the famous Algerian independence fighter and Eminent Mystic) wrote in his book *Kitãbu-l-Mawãqīf* (The Book of the Stopping Places, Alif Editions, p. 19-23) this: *"Good deeds the uninitiated servant think that they are his own are not really so: indeed such actions were accomplished by GOD HIMSELF, without any intermediary or without the servant - merely considered under his form of a creature - having played the least part therein... That is because [the ignorant servants imagine that] "their" deeds are truly fulfilled by them - and not by GOD - that the LORD attributes such deeds to them according to their belief in saying*: "Those who exult in what they have brought about". *In spite of their ignorance, such people would like however to be praised and rewarded by GOD... although them having not actually performed anything that would make them deserve such a favour since there could be no other Doer except GOD - be His Glory celebrated!....As for the Elite of the servants to whom GOD has removed their veil they are no longer disconcerted by GOD's ascribing them some deeds...Thus addressing our Master Muhammad -Peace and Blessings be upon him- the LORD told him* "When thou threwest (a handful of dust to the unbelieving faction), it was not thy act, but GOD's" (viii. 17).

101

750- O my Brother! Whenever thou realise fully what has been decreed by the LORD, accept it and behave resolutely according to such a Decree

751- And neither lose hope because of a mistake nor let thy abundant good deeds go to thy head

752- But stay within the limits of fear of GOD (_khawf_) and hope in GOD (_rajã_); because alternating these two feelings is undoubtedly the best frame of mind for a believer

753- However, the Masters advised us to nourish hope rather than fear at the point of death

754- Because it has been said that GOD's Decision [Salvation or Chastisement] is taken according to the good or bad expectations of His servant

755- How many acts of worship that led their authors to self-conceit and narcissism!

756- So much so they perished, by Divine Justice, because of their immodesty and their lack of discernment

757- How many sins that led their authors to repenting and achieving eventually Heavenly Favours!

758- So much so that they went back in the Straight Path and stayed wise for the rest of their lives, by Divine Mercy

---

Speaking as well to the Prophet as to his Companions, HE enjoined them "Fight them, and GOD will punish them by your hands" (ix. 14). _Addressing now to the Companions only, HE brought them to reality_ "It is not ye who slew them; it was GOD"(viii. 17) _notwithstanding that, if we strictly confine ourselves to the perceptible appearances, it was them who fought... So is the Truth; whether people acknowledge it or ignore it doesn't alter it the slightest bit ..."_

759- Indeed GOD's Plan appears very subtle and incomprehensible to any that endeavours to meditate on His Acts

760- "He draweth the day [of forgiveness] out of the night [of sinning] as He draweth the night [of self-conceit] out of the day [of worshipping]"[89]
761- Never fail to honour a covenant in regard to religion thou hast undertook before the MAJESTIC[90]

---

[89]This is a paraphrase of the verse iii. 27:"*[O GOD!] Thou causest the Night to gain on the Day. And Thou causest the Day to gain on the Night; Thou bringest the Living out of the Dead, and Thou bringest the Dead out of the Living...*" Let us admire the genius of the figurative interpretation of this verse in this particular situation. We may also quote on that instance the following verse which reveals how subtle the Divine Manifestations may be: "*HE Who produces for you fire out of the green tree*"(xxxvi. 80). Here is its *tafsīr* (exegesis) by the Emir Abd-el-Kader (p. 15-16): "*This verse is intended to make you realise the Perfection of GOD's Mightiness and Wonderful Wisdom. Because HE produces things out of their opposites as HE happens to conceal them into things quite alike...Out of the plant whose nature is cold and damp, HE draws fire whose nature is hot and dry!...GOD wants to show that reality to His servants so they don't confine always to rational appearances and not to rely on their knowledge, their deeds or their present situation. Because one has to mind never trusting totally material forms which differ not basically from the other creatures. Indeed GOD may well produce out of a particular form or creature an outcome that is quite opposite to the usual outcome that is expected therefrom. So they may recall that GOD remains in fact the Exclusive CREATOR and the Only One Who rules [the Universe] without His Acts depending in the least on normal and rational causes. GOD may Act, if HE so Wills, in the presence of such causes by His Wisdom or, if HE so Wills, in their absence by His Mightiness. For HE is the One Who Does what pleases HIM: drawing "good" out of what is formally "evil" as HE derives "evil" out of what is formally "good", as we may notice it often. How many favours arose from a trial! How many trials arose from a benefit! Indeed there is no other god but GOD, the WISE Whose Knowledge encompasses everything!*"
[90]Cf. Qur-ān xvi.91:"*Fulfil the Covenant of GOD when ye have entered into it, and break not your oaths after ye have confirmed them; indeed ye have made GOD your surety; for GOD knoweth all that ye do.*"

762- For aught that is lost may well be substituted [by something else] except thy CREATOR, Who that Rules all affairs[91]

763- Then do thy utmost [to always abide by thy agreements with Him]; always examine thy conscience and rid resolutely thyself of bad habits

764- Such as vices, endless and distant projects, hoarding money, prohibited actions and laziness

765- Watch on thy members and prevent them from committing aught that is forbidden by the ETERNAL-ABSOLUTE

766- Do always scrutinise thy own failings and try to cure them; repent thereof for fear of thy LORD

767- Endeavour to increase at the same time thy knowledge and thy deeds for the Sole Countenance of the GREAT and MAJESTIC LORD

768- For, verily, a true GOD-seeker (*Al-Murīd*) must never *seek* for anything else but the Satisfaction of the MOST GRACIOUS, whatever he may do

769- We may read in the book written by our Great Sheikh Al-Mukhtār, the Shining Light, the Noble related to the Kuntiyu family, this maxim:

770- *"Seeking for rest in this deceptive world will entail remorse and disgrace on the Resurrection Day"*

771- So never be deluded by people's flattering speech: *"This man is assuredly amongst the most clear-sighted and purest believers!"*

---

[91]Man is so "clever" than he always manage somehow to make up for any material or emotional loss with some palliative, but what about the *loss* of GOD's Satisfaction- which "palliative" can make up for it?

772- Never be deluded by GOD's Nobleness which concealed thy defects before people [so much so they hold thee in high esteem]

773- Never be deluded by their advantageous opinions and their respect for thee, for little do they *really* know about thee

774- Never be deluded by their coming from remote places to solicit thy assistance in knowledge matters,

775- Or their visits to obtain thy blessings or thy protection against dangers

776- Because such people are not in the least aware of thy secret or even obvious defects

777- Never be mistaken by thy LORD's Nobility, by His Kindness and His Infinite Compassion

778- Feel modest and embarrassed before thy LORD, the ALL-KNOWING; indeed lacking sense of modesty and of humility when one is conscious of His Perfect Knowledge is a proof of false-heartedness

779- Do thy utmost and rely on His Grace but never on thy sole effort and fear Him only

780- Turn all thy aspiration towards [GOD], the Only TRUTH - *may He be Exalted!* - and not towards the creatures

781- Because perfect discernment and keen penetration of spiritual aspects (Baṣīra)[92] is like eyesight: the slightest speck can prevent it from perceiving

---

[92]The notion of Baṣīra belong to the Ṣūfī terminology; that is miraculous sense of penetration of inward realities only Godly persons are endowed with...

782- Anything that has been created and which is different from GOD HIMSELF can prevent the Lights of knowledge from entering the heart, if such a thing engrosses the heart

783- Indeed escaping from all the dangerous delusions has always been, from time immemorial, amongst the hardest things![93]

784- Because downfall may derive as well from knowledge as from ignorance - so asserted it the 'Ulemã

785- It happens sometimes a man being misled by his knowledge, his generosity or his holy war (*Jihãd*)

786- ...If he aims, for instance, through his far-reaching erudition people saying: *"No doubt that such-and-such is the most learned person of this generation"*

787- Thus such a person would indulge in conveying here and there numerous information and bookish accounts without even anyone asking for his "lights"

788- In so doing, he would wander among the Scholars so as to gather enough teachings enabling him to master the different branches of science and to be the top of his generation

789- ...So as to confound any opponent daring to discuss or to argue with him!

790- Whereas the most beneficial knowledge to the heart is, of a certain
- Science of 'Ubũdiyyah, which is the knowing of the duties ascribed to the servant in respect with his LORD and how to fulfil them all,

---

[93]*Cf.* Qur-ãn lxxxii. 6: *"O man! What has seduced thee from thy LORD MOST BENEFICENT?"*

- Science of *Rubūbiya*, which is the knowing of the realities relating to GOD's Absolute Sovereignty

791- [Regarding still this crucial subject about delusions], thou may see some people persevering in giving generously their fortune to the needy without watching their spending

792- ...While aiming only thereby others saying: " *What a generous man! Never does he keep something for him"*

793- Such a person will then grow used to feed the poor and the indigent, and will shower with gifts as well youngsters as elders

794- ...Though he would keep tight-fistedly his money and would never make the least gift were it not public praises - woe to him!

795- Others have been deluded by their "holy war" (*Jihād*), because they wage war against human beings

796- They set themselves against their fellow creatures and make regular assaults in the sole order to gain more glamour and more spoils of war

797- Thus they pretend *raising* GOD's Word whereas their sole objective is *rising* to fame and not anything else!

798- So they come back from their so-called "*Jihād*" covered with sins and a host of misdeeds with all their troops

799- Some other people have been deluded by their pilgrimage in GOD's House (the *Ka'ba*); little do they comprehend

800- They go to the Holy Places in extorting illicitly Muslims' properties through corrupt public authorities

801- One may see them rushing over their doors in quest of plentiful provisions

802- So they provide themselves with ill-acquired goods and leave for the Blessed Places[94]

803- One of them may happen to forget just a single obligatory act of the Pilgrimage (*far*d) - out of tiredness for instance - that will be enough to nullify his deed[95]

804- On his return from the Mecca, he would begin to exult and to pride himself amongst people on having performed a deed which has not been accomplished by many of his generation

805- Thinking he will be imparted all kinds of fine Benefits on the Last Day whereas he will get naught but disappointment on such a Day

806- He certainly ignores that it would have been far better for him to stay at home and to muse longingly over the Holy Places!

807- Some others have been deluded by Satan - *may GOD shield us from his Mighty Snare* -

808- ...In driving them unto exaggerated asceticism, excessive self-restraint and tendency to deliver endless sermons and admonitions at any circumstance

---

[94]This is an allusion to the Koranic verse (ii. 197) which shows how such people are thoughtless:"...*And whatever good ye do, (be sure) GOD knoweth it. And take a provision (with you) for the journey [of Pilgrimage], but the best of provisions is right conduct* (Taqwā), *so fear Me, o ye that are wise.*" So instead of providing themselves with *Taqwā Lāhu-l-'Azīm* (right conduct and fear of GOD MOST HIGH) such inconsequent folk choose to amass illicit money, up to leaving for the *H*ajj!

[95]Whereas a virtuous pilgrim may be granted pardon by the Divine Mercy. Cf. Qur-ān xxiv. 39: "*But the Unbelievers, their deeds are like a mirage in sandy deserts, which the man parched with thirst mistakes for water, until when he comes up to it, he finds it to be nothing: but he finds GOD there, and GOD will pay him his account: and GOD is swift in taking account.*"

809- One may see them refusing to eat publicly - in spite of that being quite lawful - so that people say: "*How temperate [and virtuous] this man is!*"

810- Such poor scoundrels know not that such a vice is in fact a malignant "tumour" which has taken root in their very hearts

811- Consuming lawful and pure goods is surely more *praise*worthy than seeking for *praises* so perfidiously

812- For in naught people's praises will profit one of them as long as he brings himself upon the Divine Wrath

813- And, conversely, people's blames will harm him in naught as long as GOD regards him as clear-sighted[96]

814- Using licit goods and stopping oneself from pursuing glamour, for GOD's Sake, is indeed more meritorious [than such a *tartufferie*]

815- O my Brother! Whatever thou accept, do it to satisfy thy LORD, the ETERNAL-ABSOLUTE

816- And whatever thou refuse - material goods and so - do it in fearing of His Wrath

817- True asceticism (*Zuhd*) is just what we already defined in the first part[97]

818- If thou wish to be self-restrained, endeavour first to always comply with Islamic Law (*Shari'a*)[98]

---

[96]Cf. Qur-ân xxxv. 2-3: "*What GOD out of His Mercy doth bestow on mankind none can withhold: what He doth withhold, none can grant, apart from Him: and He is the Exalted in Power, Full of Wisdom. O men! Remember the grace of GOD unto you! Is there a Creator, other than GOD, to give you sustenance from heaven or earth? There is no god but He: how then are ye perverted?*"

[97]Cf. verse 697: " *True asceticism consists in ceasing to aiming in one's heart worldly purpose for GOD's Holy Face...*" and the following verses.

819- Some of such preachers recommend people to make a great effort while themselves stay very idle

820- Some of them warn solemnly against transgressing whereas themselves never cease sinning[99]

821- They recommend others to act in sincerity and purity whereas themselves are always performing ostentatious deeds[100]

822- Some pour forth brilliant and *convincing* sermons whereas themselves are not in the least *convinced* by their speeches

823- Some others have been deluded by their studies and their constant revision - fearing to show deficiencies [if questioned about religious matters] -

824- Some else by their great number of disciples or good advice [they keep on giving people]

825- While themselves have not yet purified their hearts from vices such as arrogance, hatred and other numerous failings

826- However they think they are raised to lofty degrees over the "ordinary mortals" by the LORD!

827- ...Owing to the guidance towards GOD they are providing people - no doubt that such persons are plunged in deep sleep and do not awake at all!

---

[98]Which forbids solemnly hypocrisy and with which any Muslim has to comply first (*Cf.* verse 83)

[99]*Cf.* Qur-ân ii. 44: "*Do ye enjoin right conduct on the people, and forget (to practise it) yourselves, and yet ye study the Scripture? Will ye not understand?*"

[100]*Cf.* Qur-ân iv. 142: "*The hypocrites- they seek to deceive GOD but it is GOD Who deceive them, when they stand up to prayer, they stand without earnestness, to be seen of men, but little do they hold GOD in remembrance.*"

828- Their hearts have gone off the Right Way and they understand not that GOD, the MOST HIGH

829- ...May sometimes uphold or make His Religion progress through the help of a villain!

830- Their so-called knowledge has deluded them and what they are relying on is *not* GOD - no real effort are they making indeed!

831- Well! In what use may a sickle be to a hungry person who consents not to go to the fields and to weed therein?

832- O Dear Friend! Is it useful to a thirsty man to have in his possession a rope and a buckle as long as he will be reluctant to go to the well and to draw water therefrom?

833- Wilt thou be exempted from the Obligation of Pilgrimage just because of thy having sold some provisions to a pilgrim?

834- Does it suffice - o my Brother! - to always perform ablutions without ever praying?

835- In what use is for thee a sword thou spend thy time in sharpening but which thou wilt never cut something with or fight? - *[do tell me], o Dear Companion!*

836- Alas! Thorough knowledge of several medicines will never avail to an ill person

837- ...As long as he uses not one of them to struggle against the disease which is sapping him - yea! - even if he has cured thousands and thousands of men with such drugs!

838- Whenever thou get more knowledge without thy becoming more upright and more detached of worldly goods

839- ...Know that thy progress is *negative* for thou hast thereby got farther from GOD - as quoted from a *ḥadīth* of the Holy Messenger

840- *May [GOD], Who has Sent him, impart His Peace and His Blessings upon him, as his Family and his Companions that are Elected-*

841- Indeed only an ignoramus would go hunting without any kind of arm

842- Because such a behaviour is an unseemly attitude vis-à-vis GOD, the TRUE KING of every king

843- ...[And a breach of] the Heavenly Laws He ordained to rule His Kingdom - as we will demonstrate further[101]

844- Then never go hunting unarmed and never arm thyself without ever going hunting[102]

845- But take thou thy arm and [betake thyself to the bush] and make thy utmost [to bring some game back home] - *so wilt thou reach thy aim*

846- Escaping from all the dangerous delusions is - *I do swear it by my LORD's Life!* - amongst the hardest things in the world

---

[101]This comparison is explained by the fact that the Sheikh considered any knowledge which is not put into practice in order to achieve its true purpose -worshipping duly GOD- as an impropriety and a lack of *Kasb* (consequent using of rational means) since GOD has ordained that adequate means must be used to achieve their corresponding normal outcomes...(see verses. 1036 to 1056 for other developments) *Cf.* Qur-ān lxii. 5: "*The similitude of those who were entrusted with the (obligations of) Taurat, but who subsequently failed in those (obligations), is that of a donkey which carries huge tomes (but understands them not). Evil is the similitude of people who falsify the signs of GOD: and GOD guides not people who do wrong.*"

[102]Never try to worship -or to achieve some aim- without a definite knowledge - or without using its normal means. Likewise never seek for knowledge without its subsequent putting into practice.

847- *We seek refuge in the MOST GRACIOUS from delusions and from aught that can lead unto ruin*

848- Our great Sheikh Al-Ghazāli, the Renowned Reformer of Islam, has given us clear and thorough remarks about

849- Refer to his main work "*Iḥyā 'Ulūmi-d-Dīn*" (The Revival of Religious Sciences) thou wilt find that prose work really exhaustive

850- Most of man's failings originate in fact from his natural self-esteem which makes him fear criticisms and love praises

851/852- As for the love of this ephemeral world, let us enumerate here four of its "symptoms" - *mind to stay far off them all*
   ❶ Greediness for wealth,
   ❷ Fondness of eating,
   ❸ Penchant for vain chattering
   ❹ Inclination for excessive sleeping

853- Any that is fond of one of these - without any valid constraint[103]-

854- ...Is considered as loving this fleeting life; because wealth, as far as it is concerned, leads [most of the times] unto arrogance and ill-founded self-assurance; money distracts man [from seeking for the Etrenal Light] as sleep makes people forget[104]

---

[103] Some possible excuses of such habits may be, for instance, seeking for wealth aiming sincerely and solely thereby the progress of religion- or for some other reason praiseworthy before GOD-, illness which may lead to compelling needs as bulimia and so.

[104] Cf. Qur-ān c. 6-11: "*Truly Man is, to the LORD, ungrateful. And to that (fact) he bears witness (by his deeds). And violent is he in his love of wealth. Does he not know, - when that which is in the graves is scattered abroad and that which is (locked up) in (human) breasts is made manifest- that their LORD had been Well-acquainted with them, (even to) that Day?*" See also Qur-ān xc. 5-7: "*Doth [Man] think that none hath power over him? He may say (boastfully): "Wealth have I squandered in abundance!" Thinketh he that none beholdeth him?*"

855- As for immoderate eating that hardens the heart [and makes it less "sensitive" to adoration][105]

856- Speaking too much makes the servant heedless and diverts him from remembering the MAJESTIC, so does it cause harm

857- Do know that the best provision man can keep in store here below is disregard for material goods and a heart deeply detached of worldly affairs (*Zuhd*)

858- Indeed, any that is described as a true ascetic has been granted the most laudatory quality!

859- One may count among the happy outcomes [of asceticism] peace of mind and rest in the Two Houses[106]

860- Those who have turned definitely aside from worldly perishable things are, of a surety, the *true kings*[107] - *doubt not about!*

861- They are those who have really contemplated [the Truth] and have reflected soundly; they have meditated thoroughly over Immutable Realities - so are they imparted Pre-eminence

862- It has been said in a Prophetic ḥadīth that: "*The least happy inhabitant of Paradise*

863- ...*Will have at his service one thousand servants and will marry seventy-eight Pure Maidens*"[108]

---

[105]*Sūfis* are especially severe as far as uncontrolled feeding is concerned; so are they for the inordinate satisfaction of our other basic needs. Man has to be extremely abstemious and to keep self-restrained so as not to "block" his senses and not to prevent the Divine Light one draws from adoration from illuminating his heart...

[106]Here below and in the Hereafter

[107] Is there a greater king than one who has been rid of any kind of concern about this present life? Who that keeps perfectly serene or even *pleased* before hardships?

864/870- Amongst the kinds of reasoning which may drive unto *Zuhd* let us enumerate five ones - *mentioned by the Connoisseur [of Taṣawwuf]:*

❶ Deep reflection about the fleetingness of this world and its endless worries which lead unto vices and prevent from remembering GOD,

❷ Becoming aware that love for this present life lowers man before our LORD[109]

❸ And that withdrawing from it (*Zuhd*) brings closer to GOD - *never rush lustfully towards it! -*

❹ And that *Zuhd* will induce Lofty Degrees before GOD - *what a fine Aim!* - when "medals will be awarded" Tomorrow, when the creatures will stand in a trying Wait, when all will feel scared and sorrowful, when explanations for the use of the advantages granted by GOD will be asked

❺ Snapping one's fingers at worldly affairs brings also GOD's Satisfaction and secures from His Wrath as from any source of anguish

871- Had just asceticism the virtue to lead man unto GOD's Infinite Satisfaction, that should be enough to urge humankind thereto

---

[108]The reason for this digression is to show the Splendour of Eternal Life so as to urge men unto turning aside this vile world for the Next One whose Tremendous Realities are quite matchless. *Cf.* Qur-ān xvi.96: " *What is with you must vanish: what is with GOD will endure. And We will certainly bestow, on those who patiently persevere, their reward according to the best of their actions.*" *Cf.* also Qur-ān ix. 38: "*O ye who believe! What is the matter with you, that, when ye are asked to go forth in the Cause of GOD, ye cling heavily to the earth? Do ye prefer the life of this world to the Hereafter? But little is the comfort of this life, as compared with the Hereafter.*"

[109]*Cf.* Qur-ān xvi.106-107: "*On them is Wrath from GOD, and theirs will be a dreadful Chastisement. This because they love the life of this world better than the Hereafter: and GOD will not guide those who reject Faith.*"

CHAPTER 2

The Serious Vices

872- Do know that vices - *may GOD impart us perpetual Safety against them all in the Two Houses -*

873- ...Are sins which entail the hardening of the heart and its debasement

874- A great number of vices lead any that is sullied with to perdition, to ṭard (repelling from GOD's Neighbourhood), to ḥirmān (deprivation of spiritual favours) and enmity

875- Their awful outcomes will appear abruptly to their author just before death - *there is no doubt about*

876- Any misfortune that strikes such a person during his lifetime is in fact a chastisement of GOD, the ONE, [and not the kind of hardship occurring in a virtuous man's life]

877- And whatever he might be imparted as goods and delights here below are just a subject of pride proceeding from the Plan of the MASTER of the Throne, yea! - *naught else*

878- This, conversely to the Advantages given to the Righteous

I urge thee to never consider flippantly a sin, as trifling as it may appear, but return rapidly to the ETERNAL-ABSOLUTE

879- ...In repenting sincerely and in expiating thy misdeed

880- ...Through Ṣalāt 'alā Nabī (Calling for Blessings upon our dear Prophet) - *may the ONE ensure him Peace and Salvation for aye, as to his Family and Companions-*

881- Can likewise be of use [to atone for thy sin] spending nights in worship and piety, as doing services to the Virtuous and Upright Persons

882- Sitting with the Saintly Men for the Countenance of the MAKER - *Glory to Him!* - or saying a great number of *Istighfār* [pleas of forgiveness]

883- ...Mostly the finest and most famous of them[110], or saying a lot of *Tasbīẖ*[111] or meditating [can help in repentance]

884- However preference is given to *Ṣalāt 'alā Nabī* (Calling for Blessings upon the Prophet) owing to its efficiency[112] - *as conveyed by the Accredited Reporter*

---

[110] Called *Saydu-l-Istighfār:* "The Flower of Pleas for Forgiveness" (*Cf.* verse 1527, plea 24)

[111]Glorification to GOD: "*Subhānah Lāh*"(Glory to GOD!)

[112] The Holy Prophet represents for the True Knowers far more than a simple human insofar he embodies the "Bridge" through which GOD deals with His creation; one of the reasons why he incarnate the Sign *Par Excellence* of his Infinite Mercy. *Cf.* Qur-ān xxi:107:" *We sent thee as a Mercy for all creatures.*" (See also note 71).

The Different Kinds of Vices

885- The Master in *Taṣawwuf* [Al-Yadālī] divide up the vices into two sorts:

❶ Visible vices

❷ Hidden vices

Title 1

VISIBLE VICES

886- Know thou that apparent vices are quite unlawful; *do thou repent for having lapsed into*

887/891- It is mandatory upon any person recognised as accountable for his actions (*Mukallaf*) to avoid, for fear of the MAJESTIC LORD of Mankind, such vices as
  a- Scandalmongering,
  b- Slander,
  c- Untruthfulness,
  d- Being pessimist and biased against others,
  e- Falsity,
  f- Turpitude,
  g- Any useless speech or act,
  h- Walking towards prohibitions,
  i- Looking at indecencies,
  j- Any unseemly remarks,
  k- Sinning with one's sex,
  l- ...Or through any other member[113],
  m- Lewd remarks

---

[113]Cf. Qur-ān xxxvi. 65: *"That Day shall We set a seal on their mouths. But their hands will speak to Us, and their feet bear witness to all that they did."*

892/895- It is as well forbidden

    n- To write what is unlawful

    o- To listen to it

    p- or to use it;

    q- It is positively prohibited to shed the blood

    r- ...or to misappropriate the good of a human being, be he a Muslim or not

    s- Treating coldly or turning aside from thy fellow Muslim for a reason not valid before Islamic Law (*Shari'a*) - *avoid all of these*

    t- It is also interdicted to despise a Believer,

    u- To ridicule him,

    v- To behave hypocritically with him,

    w- Or to betray him,

    x- It is neither permitted to plot against a Muslim

    y- Nor to argue inordinately with him,

    z- or any other wrong-deed likely to spoil social relationship

Title 2

HIDDEN VICES

896- As for hidden vices, they are defects which affect the Soul *herself*, wherever they may be found

897- Any such that is wallowing therein will have a painful and inauspicious death if he repents not before GOD

898- *We seek refuge in the MOST GRACIOUS from such vices, from the evil of Satan and from aught that will entail ordeals*

899- Such vices will transform themselves into scorpions and snakes after death

900- They entail a chastisement more grievous than that caused by apparent vices, because of their originating from the Soul *herself*

901- So, giving up Godly *Interdictions* is assuredly more meritorious than fulfilling Heavenly *Prescriptions* - as we hold it from the Masters

902- Hidden vices, as manifold as they may be, can be divided into three sorts - *be thou shrewd!*

903- [❶ The insubordination of the Soul]: know that human Soul has been shaped with strong aversion for any act of worship liable to satisfy GOD

904- She is, by nature, keen on resting and on pleasure although this runs counter to GOD's perfect adoration

905- [❷ Imperfections which besmirch man's worship]: if man strives hard to triumph over her and succeed in acting, the Soul will react in debasing his deeds with some imperfections until their annulment

906- A result of this is the spoiling of one's *Tawḥīd* [114], because such vices [like ostentation and the like] are a kind of subtle *Shirk* [115] - *mind thou to stay upright*

907- [❸ Self-conceit]: if man escapes from those traps, the Soul will try then to assure him of his merit until he lapses into self-conceit; so will he bring ruin upon himself [116]

---

[114]The keen sense of GOD's Unity which has to be magnified by any act of the Muslim. *Tawḥīd* represents the core of Faith in Islam...

[115]The fact of assigning partners to GOD which is quite the reverse of *Tawḥīd*. Ostentation -and the like- is considered through a Prophetic *ḥadīth* as being equivalent to "hidden *Shirk*" (*Shirk Khāfī*) due to the fact that who that is acting showily has *de facto* substituted people or other considerations for GOD in his heart...(May GOD preserve us thereof!) *Cf.* Qur-ān iv. 48: "*GOD forgiveth not that partners should be set up with Him; but He forgiveth anything else, to whom He pleased; to set up partners with GOD is to devise a sin most heinous indeed.*"

[116]Compare these different "assaults" of the Soul with Satan's Snares as described in verse 667-684. This implies that the Soul is one of Satan's "Trojan Horses" with which he combats man...

908- O Shrewd Man! Do realise that thou wilt never get nearer to GOD, the MAJESTIC, until thou overcome these three different stages

909- [So I do advise thee first] to become aware of their existence and what relates thereto - *this is unavoidable* - then to get over them in curing the corresponding vices

910- Indeed this is the greatest objective a servant can wish to achieve so as to get closer to his LORD - *waken thou!*

911- Endeavour to know all of them, o my Friend! , by going and seeing frequently the great Sheikhs who will give thee judicious advice

912- I also suggest thee to keep company with sincere and trustworthy friends [so they may show thee frankly thy failings] and not to ignore thy enemies' remarks [likely to enlighten thee by their wicked but pertinent remarks]

913- As for the manner to get rid of all these vices, that is turning resolutely towards our LORD in humility

914- For " it is far more reasonable to appeal to the master of the dog rather than trying to tame it by thyself"

915/918-[May likewise help in curing hidden vices] absolute sincerity in striving against one's Soul -so as to gain the advantages deriving therefrom in using as "arms"

 a- Accustoming thyself to hunger,

 b- Depriving thy Soul of worldly pleasures and rejoicing she never ceases lusting after,

 c- Weighing her down with tough acts of worship,

 d- Keeping often company with Saintly Men in order to imitate them,

 e- Consuming only pure and licit goods, nay those of doubtful lawfulness or those that are quite illicit or alike

919- O Dear Friend! Eat what pleases thee, no doubt thou wilt act accordingly. Choose whomever pleases thee as a companion, no doubt thou wilt be like such a person[117]

920- [May also help in curing the heart debasement] fleeing every dens of vice and every sinning places, and seeking for an upright companion who worships the LORD

921- So, to be secured from Lady Hind[118] and from her acolytes, one has to beware of ever going down to her dark valleys

---

[117]If you feed yourself on illicit goods, whatever your intention may be you will do wrong deeds. If you feed yourself on lawful goods, whatever your intention may be you will do good deeds. If you strike an intimate friendship with bad company, there will be every chance you lapse into transgression some day.

Cf. also Qur-ān xxv. 27-29: *"The Day that the wrong-doer will bite at his hands, he will say, "Oh! Would that I had taken a (straight) path with the Messenger! Ah! Woe is me! Would that I had never taken such a one for a friend! He did lead me astray from the Message (of GOD) after it had come to me! Ah! The satan is but a traitor to man!""*

[118] Female Arabic name embodying the seduction of this world or of Satan and so. The same with Lubna, Layla, Salma, Sũda... This is the reason why the pronoun "she" is commonly used to refer to this world(*Dunyã*) and Lust (*Nafs*) which are feminine nouns in Arabic...

Other Vices

and their corresponding remedies

922- Here are certain other vices explained in detail and their respective remedies; [*listen thou carefully to these "prescriptions" of mine, Dear Patient*]

a- **Arrogance** (*kibr*)

923- Of a certain, arrogance is the most serious vice inasmuch as it consumes entirely the servant's faith

924- As for the other vices [connecting thereto], they entail the spoiling of the deeds

925/926- Among these we count:
    ❶ Natural shame and *amour-propre* [which incites man unto disliking to be corrected]
    ❷ Concealing or dismissing the truth [lest one should be belittled before people]
    ❸ Scorning every human being - *give up thou haughtiness!*

927- The remedy of arrogance consists in always calling in one's mind that we are physiologically shaped like every human being and we are not in the least primarily different

928- Thou art superior to none, my Brother! since thou know not which fate is held in store for thee after death

929- One has also to bethink oneself and to remember GOD's Word which threatens any arrogant person with a grievous chastisement

930- One must recall that it is such a vice which ruined Satan, the Cursed - *we seek refuge in the HELPER against him and against any sort of pride-*

931- Do remember that thou wert formerly naught but a vile sperm drop[119] and even now thou art constrained to bear any sort of soils inside thy body!

932- Once in the grave thou wilt become [as renowned as thou might be] a rotten, stinking, abominable and trivial cadaver!

933- Ye are, all of you, simply "sons of Adam"[120] and recall that this latter was created from lowly earthy clay!

b- Self-conceit (*'Ujb*)

934- [Self-conceit is another serious vice] whose remedy consists, for the servant, in knowing that

935- ...He is not in reality the *true* and *ultimate* author of "his" good deeds, for he only represents a tool in GOD's "Hands" [Who have urge him on to acting], and in knowing that "his" deeds are liable to be not accepted

936- Its cure consists also in knowing that he has never ceased performing inappropriately his duty [in respect with GOD's GREATNESS]

---

[119]Cf. Qur-ān lxxv. 36-40: *"Does Man think that he will be left uncontrolled, (without purpose)? Was he not a drop of sperm emitted (in lowly form)? Then did he become a leach-light clot; then did (GOD) make and fashion (him) in due proportion. And of him He made two sexes, male and female. Has not He, (the same), the power to give life to the dead?"*
[120]Descendants of Adam *i. e.* humankind.

937- And that he has not yet fulfilled even the equivalent of a *naqīr*[121] about what is incumbent on him vis-à-vis the MAJESTIC LORD; not has he performed the equivalent of a *fatīl*[122] or even that of an atom!

938- [Do also help in curing self-conceit] the knowing that whoever puts his trust in anything but GOD HIMSELF shall be forsaken by that very thing and be humiliated on the Day of Distress

939- Because numerous acts of worship are all at once nullified at the slightest evocation by who has performed them

940- It is not proper that a servant of GOD speaks in praise of the adoration he is dedicating to his LORD, That Who holds all Favours

c- **Love for fame** (*Sum'a*) and **ostentation** (*Riyā*)

941- As for the definition of *Sum'a* that is - *according to the Accredited Source* - narrating to others one's fine deeds

942- ...Just for earthly purpose such as winning people's praises and admiration; this vice has indeed some similarities to ostentation

943- As regarding ostentation it consists in performing good deeds and aiming solely thereby people's esteem

944- ...Or in order to acquire earthly advantages - as wealth - or to ward off some damage one is fearing [in disregard for the Divine Mightiness]

---

[121] See note below.

[122] *"The lexicographical distinction made between the words "Naqīr" and "Fātīl"...is: the "Naqīr" is the external husk of the date whilst the "Fātīl" is the small groove of its stone."*(*Cf.* verses 75-76 of "Jawhār-n-Nafīz" (The Precious Jewel) written by the Sheikh)

945- However there is a divergence amongst the Masters as to know if who that acts for a worldly purpose while having a laudable intention in his inmost heart is acting ostentatiously[123]

946- Concerning any act which has been done without any earthly aim [and that has been performed for the sole Sake of GOD], we call it _Ikhlās_ (Absolute Purity)[124] - _do fear the outcomes [of ostentation]_

947- But as for any such that is aiming inwardly the creatures through his good deeds [and whose profound objective is not the LORD], his act is tainted by ostentation

948- Yea! Was he acting in secrecy[125]. As for the servant who acts quite conversely, he is ranked amongst the _Mukhlisīn_ (Sincere Worshippers)

949- This even if his act has been performed publicly, because people's attendance has no effect in his heart

950- Even deeds which have been accomplished by a zealous worshipper with the sole view to attain GOD's Neighbourhood

---

[123] The question concerns, for instance, a man that strives hard to feed his family in order to assist them even if he is not animated by a strictly godly purpose. Some Doctors consider that his intention is in itself noble enough to save him from ostentation. Whereas others, more rigorous, persist on laying stress on the importance of the direct quest of GOD's Satisfaction through every action.

[124] The concept of _Ikhlās_ (which is the quite opposite of ostentation and giving partners to GOD (_Shirk_)) is the most highly valued virtue in Islam as we may constantly realise it throughout the Holy Scriptures. _Cf._ Qur-ān xxxix. 2-3: _"Verily it is We Who have revealed the Book to thee in Truth: so serve GOD, offering Him sincere devotion. Is it not to GOD that sincere devotion is due? "_ and several other similar verses and _ahādith_.

[125] This case concerns, for instance, who that acts discreetly or in some retired place while wishing in his inmost heart that his deeds may be disclosed one day and publicly known so as to be praised for his discretion and his concern not to lapse into ostentation... How tortuous can the twists and turns of man's consciousness be!

(*Haḍratu-Lāh*) are likewise ranked among the ostentatious acts by the Elect[126]!

951- ...As well as acts of worship performed just to derive therefrom the pleasure of adoration or acts which are fulfilled in the sole concern to get nearer to GOD (*Wusūl*)!

952- ...Or to be esteemed for one's godliness and miracles - *which are in fact granted by our LORD, Who that bestows His Unbounded Grace on His servants*

953- Such behaviours as well as any other deeds of worship whose basic and deepest object is earning people's admiration and respect are called " inconspicuous ostentation" - *grasp thou this*

954- Belong also to that kind of hidden *riyā* the habit of bending modestly one's head when meeting people whereas one feels not in the least humble [before GOD's Majesty]

955- Like so the fact of giving up certain beneficial acts of worship because of people[127] or declining false-modestly their thanks in order to be praised *more*

---

[126]This would seem really paradoxical to the "common servants" since such aim appear quite praiseworthy at first glance... But it is fully understandable considered from *Sūfī* Masters' point of view. Knowing that for those out-of-the-ordinary worshippers, true subjection and servitude to GOD MOST HIGH implies the complete emptying out of the heart any purpose and interest besides GOD *HIMSELF*. This, as valuable as such purposes may seem to be at first glance. So the sole valid aim remains, for them, GOD's Holy Face. Thus goes the famous saying "*Hasanatu-l-Abrār Sayyiātu-l-Muqarrabīn*" (The Good Deeds of the Virtuous are considered as sins by the Neighbouring Elite), summing up the idea that faults which are overlooked regarding the " troops " will be regarded as punishable as far as the " officers " are concerned, because of their " sharing the Secrets of the Powers that be "... *Cf.* Qur-ãn vi. 162: "*Say:* "Truly, my prayer and my service of sacrifice, my life and my death, are (all) for GOD, the CHERISHER of the Worlds.""

956- The therapy of these two vices [seeking for celebrity and ostentation] consists in always calling in one's mind that everything depends ultimately on GOD

957- Indeed no creature can get something by *his own self*, then how could he entail some benefit to another creature by *his own self*?

958- O my Friend! Do recall the bitter warning of the MOST GRACIOUS concerning these two vices[128]

---

[127] This concerns who that withdraws from doing a good deed lest one should be praised thereof, for instance. This is considered as ostentatious by the Sheikh because any giving up as well as any undertaking must derived from the sole concern to seek GOD's Holy Face...

[128]*Cf.* Qur-ān cvii. 4-6: *"So woe to the worshippers who are neglectful of their prayers, those who (want but) to be seen"* As a piece of admonition about delusions and ostentatious deeds, let us mention this following fearsome *Hadith Qudsi*, related by Muslim (also by at-Tirmidhi and an-Nasa'i) on the authority of Abu Hurayrah (may GOD be pleased with him), who said: *"I heard the Messenger of GOD (PBH) say:* *"The first of people against whom judgment will be pronounced on the Day of Resurrection will be a man who died a martyr. He will be brought and GOD will make known to him His favours and he will recognize them. [The Almighty] will say: And what did you do about them? He will say: I fought for you until I died a martyr. He will say: You have lied - you did but fight that it might be said [of you]: He is courageous. And so it was said. Then he will be ordered to be dragged along on his face until he is cast into Hell-fire. [Another] will be a man who has studied [religious] knowledge and has taught it and who used to recite the Quran. He will be brought and GOD will make known to his His favours and he will recognize them. [The Almighty] will say: And what did you do about them? He will say: I studied [religious] knowledge and I taught it and I recited the Quran for Your sake. He will say: You have lied - you did but study [religious] knowledge that it might be said [of you]: He is learned. And you recited the Quran that it might be said [of you]: He is a reciter. And so it was said. Then he will be ordered to be dragged along on his face until he is cast into Hell-fire. [Another] will be a man whom GOD had made rich and to whom He had given all kinds of wealth. He will be brought and GOD will make known to his His favours and he will recognize them. [The Almighty] will say: And what did you do about them? He will say: I left no path [untrodden] in which You like money to be spent without spending in it for Your sake. He will say: You have lied - you did but do so*

959- Indeed any person who is acting showily may be compared to a gold digger who found a giant nugget

960- …Whose price amounts to thousands and thousands of dinars but who traded it for a trifling coin!

961- Whereas he could have sold it for a fortune were he not so insane

962- Thus, though having the opportunity to obtain the ALMIGHTY's Satisfaction through his deed, the showy man declined it and chose absurdly to please some poor fellow

963- What about him if that poor fellow comes to reject him after his having been already disgraced by the ALMIGHTY?

964- Because as soon as such a fellow will be conscious that [that "valorous" man] was acting just out of ostentation there is no doubt he will disavow his deed and will despise him henceforth

965- Act thou, [o my Friend!], for Whom that will never fail to be Satisfied with thee if thou act sincerely for His Sake[129]

966- Act thou henceforth for Whom that will shield thee in the two Houses[130] from aught that frighten thee if thou win His Satisfaction

967- Act thou from now on for Whom that will suffice any such that seeks sincerely for His Countenance so much that he will no longer need anyone else

968- Act thou for Whom that will impart thee Honour and that will grant all thy wishes if thou avoid His Prohibitions

d - Envy (ḥasad), hatred (ḥiqd) and deceitfulness (Ghish)

---

that it might be said [of you]: He is open-handed. And so it was said. Then he will be ordered to be dragged along on his face until he is cast into Hell-fire."
[129]GOD MOST HIGH.
[130]Here below and the Hereafter

969- Wishing an honest Muslim lose his benefits and advantages is called _hasad_ (envy)

970- [That is assuredly an iniquitous feeling] because any person that is filled with it is strongly opposed that such advantages could entail profit or salvation for the object of his envy!

971- A jealous person is always bothered and upset by his brother's advantage; naught will ever rejoices him but his harm

972- As for the criterion of what is known as _hiqd_ (hatred) that is: treating an upright person as an enemy without any definite ground justifiable in the view of Islamic Law[131]

973- As regarding deceitfulness, it concerns who that conceals deliberately his failings [in order to dupe] any that is not aware thereof

974- …Were such failings relating to his religious practices or his everyday attitude - _as written in the Texts_

975- Struggle thou against thy hatred in strongly _hating_ it first; as thou shouldst do for all thy bad habits - _so wilt thou gain profit_

976- [Do also regret] having committed thereby what is forbidden by the MAJESTIC LORD and act thou henceforth with benevolence towards the victim of thy hatred

977- Persevere in making sincere prayers for that person without him even knowing and do thy utmost to wish him good, nay harm
978- Know that whoever hates a servant that is loved and honoured by GOD, such a person incurs the Divine Wrath

979- His heart would never cease hurting and worrying because he has set himself up as an opponent of the Infinite and Eternal Mercy!

---

[131]As an excessive and persistent mischief.

980- He would not cease behaving hostilely with that privileged person just because he feels not satisfied by such a situation [ordained yet by the ABSOLUTE LORD!]

981- Actually there are no defects more pernicious and harmful than [envy and hatred] - so never harbour a feeling of hatred for a human being

982- But love and respect anyone GOD has chosen by His Grace and avoid ever lapsing into wanton denigration

983- Never *refuse* to do him favours lest GOD should *refuse* thee His Bounties and Advantages too

e- Guilefulness (*Zayn*)

984- As for the vice called *Zayn*, it consists in displaying an attracting and estimable appearance before people whereas one's heart and mind are overrun by disreputable thoughts

985- Such a base tendency can be cured, o Dear Friend!, by regular performance of *Dhikr* in humility and reverence

986- Do brighten thy heart and make it finer instead of thy appearances, because the heart is the place whereon focuses the Sight of the LORD of humankind

987- GOD considers rather our inner features whilst the creatures content themselves with our outward appearances

988- If thou improve thy inside without caring overmuch for thy outside thou wilt gain True Splendour, that which is devoid of any artful device

989- Because whosoever succeeds in perfecting his heart will see his behaviour improving too - *thus will he attain Bliss*

f- **Other superficial attitudes**

990- Now regarding other defects, such as the pursuit of glory, of glamour and authority or the liking of competition

991- ...And any other sort of craving for eminence over people, they estrange the servant from the MOST HIGH

992- [Note however that] this is the case only if what is aimed thereby is just a worldly purpose; but [this is not condemned by the Masters] in case one seeks sincerely through such advantages the Holy Face[132]

993- As for vain rivalling in knowledge just for showing off or aiming wealth thereby,

994- Or puffing up in arrogance because of one's erudition or seeking for supremacy through religious knowledge: all of these lead surely unto ruin and loss

995- Toughest Punishments are foretold thereon - *refer thou to the Holy Text*

996- Do praise thy LORD - the MAJESTIC and MOST HIGH - if He ranked thee amongst those who put sincerely their knowledge into practice, because He had granted thee True Guidance then

g- **Relying in the creatures**

997- As for vices like servility, fearing thy fellow creatures, putting thy trust or expecting thy means of subsistence from them

998- ...Or over-complaining to them about thy misfortunes [in expecting their help]: [to cure them] know that people are unable [of bringing either good or evil] to thee; they are naught but weak creatures

---

[132]As the progress of religion...

999- Thou wilt obtain nothing in thy life but what has been ordained by the ALMIGHTY LORD [whatever thy attempts may be]

1000- For *"The Pen has got dried"*[133]; the exact portions of wealth assigned to every being are already decreed

1001- In fact the ABSOLUTE MASTER has already done with four things:
- ❶ Our life term (*Ajal*)
- ❷ Our physical shape (*Khalq*)
- ❸ Our basic nature and character (*Khuluq*)[134]
- ❹ What we will receive as means of subsistence (*Rizq*)[135]

1002- So whosoever tries to obtain anything which has not been ordained for him will wear himself out in vain, for nought shall he get!
1003- Thou wilt only obtain what pleases GOD, whatever thy efforts may be, o thou GOD-seeker!

1004- Good as well as evil comes exclusively from Him; so endeavour to comply with His Orders and to avoid His Prohibitions

---

[133]In other words "Dies of every fate are already cast"... *Cf.* Qur-ān xiii. 26: *"GOD doth enlarge, or grant by (strict) measure, the substance (which He giveth) to whomso he pleaseth."* This question of Fate and human destiny, in regard with human responsibility and will, arose very harsh debates among muslim scholars in the past. One can refer to the theological book dedicated to that question for more information.

[134]We are almost tempted to translate *khuluq* by "genetic code"...

[135]*Cf.* Qur-ān lv. 29: *"Of Him seeks (its need) every creature in the heavens and on earth: every day in (new) Splendour doth He (shine)!"* This verse is commented in Yusuf Ali's translation (note 5191): *"Every single creature depends on GOD for its needs: of all of them the CHERISHER and SUSTAINER is GOD. Seek (its needs): does not necessarily mean 'seek them in words': what is meant is the dependence: the allusion is to the Source of supply."*

1005- Had all the creatures put their efforts together in order to bring thee some benefit they will never succeed therein as long as He wills not

1006- *Mieux,* had they all together gathered to move a single atom in the Dominion of the MOST GRACIOUS

1007- ...Without His Will, soon will they realise their absolute impotence!

1008- Know that anything which affect us in our life, that is because GOD has ordained it not to miss us

1009- And [conversely] aught that miss us in our life, GOD has ordained it not to affect us

1010- Then do trust in Him and lean on Him; cease from bothering and entertaining doubts [about His Mightiness]

1011- If thou put sincerely thy trust in Him thou wilt be granted an unadulterated Satisfaction

1012- But if ever thou substitute Him for something else [and replace Him by a creature in thy heart] thou wilt bring surely thyself upon an irretrievable loss - *wilt thou not think?*

1013- Never concern thyself overmuch with wealth at the expense of GOD's Adoration lest thou shouldst be deprived of Eternal Rest and of any Intercession in the Hereafter

1014- Because [the LORD] has taken upon Himself to ensure our means of subsistence and to share them out amongst us

1015- Never be upset or feel in despair because of their shortage and may not that lead thee unto neglecting to worship duly GOD

1016- Because the MOST HIGH LORD knows perfectly about the affairs of all His creatures and not in the least is He careless

1017- He is too NOBLE to fail in His Promise and too MAJESTIC to forget or to be unable to do whatever thing

1018- Endeavour to acquire firm Faith in GOD and in His Eternal Word[136]

1019- Lift up thy entire aspiration unto [GOD], the ULTIMATE TRUTH, rely solidly on Him and never turn back toward the creatures [to satisfy thy needs]

1020- Raise not in thy heart the rich person just owing to his wealth and turn not aside from the poor person

1021- Even the Holy Prophet, the Chosen Par Excellence - *may the LORD grant him Peace and Blessings* - underwent the Divine Reproach thereof[137]

---

[136]*Cf.* Qur-ān xi. 123: "*To GOD do belong the unseen (secrets) of the heavens and the earth, and to him goeth back every affair (for decision): so worship Him: and put thy trust in Him: and thy LORD is not unmindful of aught that ye do.*"

[137]This refers to an incident to which the Sūrah lxxx ('*Abasa;* He Frowned) makes allusion. (*Cf.* intro. Yusuf Ali's translation of the Qur-ān):"*The Holy Prophet was once deeply and earnestly engaged in trying to explain the holy Qur-ān to Pagan Quraish leaders, when he was interrupted by a blind man 'Abdullāh ibn Umm-i-Muktūm, one who was also poor, so that no one took any notice of him. He wanted to learn the Qur-ān. The holy Prophet naturally disliked the interruption. Perhaps the poor man's feelings were hurt. But he whose gentle heart ever sympathised with the poor and the afflicted, got new Light from above, and without the least hesitation published this revelation (...) And the Prophet always afterwards held the man in high honour*" These are the verses in question: "*He frowned and turned away, because there came to him the blind man (interrupting). But what could tell thee but that perchance he might grow in purity? Or that he might receive Admonition, and the Reminder might profit him? As to one who regards himself as self-sufficient, to him dost thou attend; though it is no blame to thee if he grow not in purity. But as to him who came to thee striving earnestly, and with fear (in his heart) of him wast thou unmindful...*" Cf. also Qur-ān vi. 52: " *Send not away those who*

1022- O Poor Thing! Know that thou wilt obtain from such worldly goods naught but what GOD has *Himself* assigned thee thereof!

h- Man's natural fondness for praising and aversion for criticisms

1023- Thy fondness for delusive praising and thy aversion for well-founded criticisms, out of fear of shame

1024- ...Are assuredly a sign of profound ignorance and silliness; a proof of little shrewdness and a lack of clear-sightedness

1025- Whoever relies on what people say flatteringly about him - without them even knowing him really - and who comes to forget what *himself* is absolutely certain of - concerning his *own* failings - such a one is indeed a sleeping fool

i- The feeling of superiority over people

1026- Being fully convinced of one's superiority over people is amongst the most grave vices – *do know that my Friend*

1027- Being pessimist and biased against others while having a high opinion of thyself and thy deeds

1028- ...Is a sign of foolishness thou hast to cure in examining everyday thy conscience and in realising how unfair thou art

---

call on their LORD morning and evening, seeking His Face. In naught art thou accountable for them, and in naught are they accountable for thee, that thou shouldst turn them away, and thus be (one) of the unjust." See also Qur-ān xviii. 28: *"And keep yourself content with those who call on their LORD morning and evening, seeking His Face; and let not thine eyes pass beyond them, seeking the pomp and glitter of this life; nor obey any whose heart We have permitted to neglect the remembrance of Us, one who follows his own desires, and his affair has become all excess."*

1029- Be thou optimist instead and think highly of thy fellow creatures because only GOD is entitled to know exactly their fate, until the Resurrection Day

j- Heedlessness

1030- And from such diseases as lack of decisiveness, postponing endlessly good deeds performance, heedlessness and persistency in sinning

1031- ...Cure thyself in meditating on the Dreadful Chastisement [reserved to the idle] in the Coming World and on the Delights promised to those who are striving hard in adoration

1032- And call in thy mind that GOD, as far as He is concerned, is *never* heedless of *aught* thou may do, be it hidden or not

1033- And that He will some day call us unto accounts as slight as a *fatīl*[138]; He will leave out the slihgtest thing about thee, be it a great or a trifling act

1034- Know that, on the Last Day, most of the moans and the tears from Hell will originate from idle persons regretting to have lacked [in their past lives] decisiveness in worshipping duly GOD

1035- Thou know even not if thou wilt be still living tomorrow or if thou wilt be as capable of performing what thou intent as thou art *now* - thence [do give up indolence] and hasten thou to adore GOD!

k- Giving up rational efforts (*Kasb*) on the pretence of *Tawakkul*

1036- Giving up rational efforts (*Kasb*) on the pretence of having "put one's entire trust in the LORD" (*Tawakkul*), while one expects people's assistance, is an insane behaviour indeed

---

[138]*Cf.* note 176.

1037- Do know that confiding in GOD (*Tawakkul*) and making rational actions[139] are not mutually exclusive - *waste not thy time [in such a misconception]!*

1038- On that matter true *Tawakkul* consists in being deeply convinced that only the LORD of the Creation [is entitled to entail whatever effect and] to expect not thy means of subsistence from anything but Him

1039- The most proper mind-set is to combine both of these [*Tawakkul* and *Kasb*], even if there is some divergence amongst the Masters about this question

1040- [The fact is] GOD has ordained for aye that the effects *He* produces will always be connected somehow to the apparent rational causes proceeding from His creatures

1041- So He can decide freely, seeing that all the *necessary* rational causes are gathered, to use such causes as the "Gate" through which He will act; just because of His Infinite Wisdom

1042- Thus the LORD demonstrates, through such unchanging Laws[140], His Absolute Kingship and Sovereignty over the Creation - how GRAND and LOFTY He is!

1043- So any such who expects [GOD] producing some effects without "opening the Gate" of its rational causes - as, for instance, who that hopes to get nearer to Him without worshipping Him duly -

1044- ... Such a person is showing incorrectness and is behaving unseemly with his LORD; so nought shall he obtain!

---

[139]To earn one's daily bread, for instance

[140] The *'Awāid* are literally the customs by which GOD ordained that His creation will be ruled. So the rational Laws which are at work in the nature as well as the Divine Rules which deals with man's worshipping and with his fate are likewise comprised in such *'Awāid* ...

1045- The main divergence amongst the Masters is to know what is the best between *Tawakkul* and *Kasb*; however such a divergence occurs not if one is totally unable to use normal means [in which case confiding in GOD without acting is preferred of course]

1046- If there is a definite possibility to use normal means, putting one's entire trust in GOD (*Tawakkul*) is still imperative provide man can stop himself from expecting his means of subsistence from the creatures in his inner self

1047- And provide that makes not him envious, disturbed, indecisive or distressed

1048- But if in committing himself to GOD, he cannot help from turning secretly towards the creatures, the Upright Masters enjoin him to combine *Tawakkul* and the using of normal means (*Kasb*)

1049- Such an attitude consists in emptying one's heart out of any negative feeling, in enjoying such a detachment and in accomplishing due and rational actions

1050- [A definite evidence of *Kasb* relevance is] GOD commands His servants to stay far from the causes of ruin and harm

1051- ...And to devote themselves to the causes of salvation – *so mind to always eschew from what leads to Blaming*

1052- Avoiding the causes of evil means, to some extents, escaping from an ill fate [linked to wrongdoing] and coming to another fate [more favourable] decreed by the LORD of Creation[141]

---

[141]*Cf.* Qur-ān xvii. 13: "*Every man's fate we have fastened on his own neck: on the day of judgement we shall bring out for him a scroll which he will see spread open.*"
About this question of determinism, we may also read in the Qur-ān (lxxiv. 54-56): "*Nay, this surely is an admonition: let any who will, keep it in remembrance! But none will keep in remembrance except as GOD wills: He is the LORD of Righteousness, and the LORD of Forgiveness.*" and Qur-ān lxxxi. 27-29: "*Verily*

141

1053- O Dear Brother! act thou *outwardly* [to achieve thy objective] in using rational means while submitting *inwardly* thyself to GOD's Will and relying only on Him

1054- For He is Who that has created such means; confide always in Him and stand thou humbly before the "Gate" [of His Acts][142]

1055- Thus wilt thou combine *Shari'a* and *Haqīqah*[143]- this is assuredly the most balanced attitude one may adopt

1056- Giving up totally rational means is considered as an heresy [in contradiction with the Prophetic *Sunna*] but disregarding any concern for *Tawakkul* amounts to assigning partners to GOD (*Shirk*)[144]

1- Thoughtlessness

1057- Making endless and distant projects prevents the believer from repenting, hardens his heart and leads him unto laziness [of worship] and shortcomings

1058- Because such a habit drives man unto neglecting worship and unto perpetuating lenient delusions

---

this is no less than a Message to (all) the Worlds, (with profit) to whoever among you wills to go straight: but ye shall not will except as GOD wills, the CHERISHER of the Worlds." Here is Yusuf Ali's commentary of these verses (note 5996): "GOD is the CHERISHER of the Worlds, LORD of Grace and Mercy, and His guidance is open to all who have the will to profit by it. But that will must be exercised in conformity with GOD's will (verse 29). Such conformity is Islam. Verse 28 points to human free-will and responsibility; verse 29 to its limitations. Both extremes, viz.: cast-iron Determinism and an idea of chaotic Free-will, are condemned."

[142]i.e. normal means

[143] See notes corresponding to verses 732.

[144]Lacking of *Tawakkul* means neglecting to have faith in GOD's Almightiness; so the partners here are the creatures one makes play the part of the LORD...

1059- Do remember that human life is too short and, swiftly, time flies...Think thou about the Dreads of Death, o Worshipper!

1060- Thou know not even if thou art not already on the shaky brink of Ruin, with all thy grandiose dreams!

1061- Spending one's entire life into idleness or into vain activities is assuredly most detrimental - [an irretrievable Loss]

1062- [To cure such thoughtlessness] one has to bear in mind that man's lifetime is too *priceless*, so he must spend it into *precious* activities

1063- As for constant joviality and excessive liking for rest, we must repress them in thinking over [the uncertainty of the future] and in meditating on coming hardships

1064- ...As the illness which will lead us unto death, our mortal agony, the sojourn into the grave, the Great Gathering [and other hard Stages of Doomsday]- *mind thou to stay in awe for its Dreads*

1065- Be aware of the shortcomings of thy good deeds and never forget that GOD, MOST HIGH, dislikes who that exults[145]

m- The feeling of impunity

1066- Whenever thou commit a wrongdoing without GOD punishing thee forthwith and [instead of repenting] that gives thee a feeling of impunity or incites thee to persist in sinning

1067- ... Realise that such an overlook is not a sign of slackening or carelessness of the LORD - [He is indeed] too MAJESTIC [to do this]

---

[145]Cf. Qur-ãn lvii.23: " *In order that ye may not despair over matters that pass you by, nor exult over favours bestowed upon you. For GOD loveth not any vainglorious boaster.* "

1068- But that is merely [the way He acts with wrong-doers] and this way of behaving is intended to make thee feel more secure so as to lead thee where thou dost not know - *wilt not thou ask for His Forgiveness?*

1069- Any time thou feel secure from His Unfathomable Plan, know that it would be [a sign of perdition] and a sign of profound ill-appraisal of His [Mightiness] - naught else

n- Despair about the Divine Mercy (*Qunūt*)

1070- To cure thyself from losing any hope [in the Divine Pardon], do meditate on the Signs of His Boundless Grace and contemplate His Infinite Mercy[146] - *so wilt thou find consolation*

o- Bias against others

1071- Regarding now that sort of "short-sightedness" which prevents thee from becoming aware of thy own failings but that shows thee others'

1072- ... Its remedy consists in forgiving thy fellow creatures and in always concealing indulgently and kindly their shortcomings so may the LORD veil thy mistakes on the Last Day too

p- Love for this contemptible world

---

[146]GOD's Kindness over the Righteous through stories of old related in the Qur-ān , for instance, or the Countless Signs of His Bounty any sound spirit can contemplate around him, in his everyday life... About *Qunūt* (despair), the LORD teaches us: "*And who despairs of the Mercy of his LORD, but such as go astray?*" (Qur-ān xv. 56) This *Hadith Qudsi* was related by Muslim (also by al-Bukhari, an-Nasa'i and Ibn Majah), on the authority of Abu Hurayrah (may God be pleased with him), who said that the Messenger of God (PBUH) said: "*When God decreed the Creation He pledged Himself by writing in His book which is laid down with Him: My mercy prevails over my wrath.*"

1073- As for the immoderate penchant for this world - regarded as highly negligible by GOD[147] to Whom belongs True Religion -

1074- May help in curing it: meditation on its contemptible destiny and its inexorable fading; [O Man! do ask thyself]: *"Where are now the past generations?"*

1075- *"Where may be now the honours after which they were running [so greedily]? In what use are now for them the valuables [they were collecting]? Now, what about the delights they were savouring?*[148]

1076- Remember that this world is not our true home, but it is basically a place of worry and constraint [for humankind]

1077- Indeed, is showing shrewdness only he who makes it his objective to enter the Home of Eternal Sojourn[149] and who is making a great effort, night and day, to such an end

q- Conjecturing about GOD's Decision

1078- As regards the habit of wishing that GOD's Decision had been different and disagreeing with His Acts, [one has to stop behaving so] and to submit fully to His Absolute Will!

1079- Thou know not even - *o Dear Brother!* - if what thou art longing for would be *really* beneficial to thee or if it would not turn out as the cause of thy ruin

1080- ...Or if it would not entail His Wrath - *do surrender thy affairs to Him!*[150]

---

[147]Cf. Qur-ān vi. 32: *"Nothing is the life of this world but play and amusement. But best is the Home in the Hereafter, for those who are righteous. Will ye not then understand?"*

[148]Cf. Qur-ān xix.98: *"But how many (countless) generations before them have We destroyed? Canst thou find a single one of them (now) or hear (so much as) a whisper of them?"*

[149]Paradise.

r- Condescension

1081- To cure thyself from such vices as condescension and feeling proud in spending [on charity or on other praiseworthy purposes], do recall that the only One Who is actually bestowing His Favours [to the entire Creation]

1082- ... Is the BOUNTIFUL LORD! And thou art naught but *His* humble intermediary

s- Quick-temperance and Intolerance

1083- As for tendency to hotheadedness, quick-temperance, animosity and intolerance

1084- They are the features *par excellence* of Satan, the Cursed [who inoculates them to his hellhounds] - *we seek an eternal refuge in the SUPREME HELPER from him* -

1085- Their remedy consists in being fully aware that any act [which is assigned rationally and outwardly to a creature] has been *in fact* accomplished by the MAJESTIC LORD[151]

t- Impatience

1086- In case thou art excessively impatient [I advise thee to] appeal humbly to thy LORD's Assistance so He may cure thee thereof

---

[150]Cf. Qur-ān ii. 216: *"It is possible that that ye dislike a thing which is good for you, and that ye love a thing which is bad for you. Only GOD knoweth and ye know not"* and Qur-ān xvii. 11: *"Men prays for evil as fervently as he prays for good for man is given to haste."*

[151]So one has not to show excessive annoyance and irritation before people's mistakes...

1087- Because impatience may lead GOD to withdraw His favours, unto discouragement, regrets and transgression[152]

---

[152]Excessive impatience to attain lofty degrees can indeed drive the worshipper unto great haste and lack of sense of Ethics (*adab*) towards the LORD, this entailing the withdrawal of his Favours. It can also lead unto discouragement inasmuch as who that is seeking for GOD's Satisfaction may feel weary and disconcerted by the "extreme slowness" of worship outcomes. Impatience would also incite man to behaving unseemly in trying situations where perfect forbearance is required; so does it induce transgression... *Cf.* also Qur-ān lxx. 19-21: "*Truly man was created very impatient; fretful when evil touches him; and niggardly when good reaches him.*"

CHAPTER 3

Muslim Ethics
(Adab)

AND SOME BENEFICIAL PRACTICES OF
WORSHIP (*Fadãil*)

Muslim Ethics (Adab)

&

beneficial practices of worship

Part I: The Rules of *ADAB* [153]

1088- Do know - *may GOD MOST HIGH grant us the Lights of the Two Houses by His Grace -*

1089- ...That the finest Ornament man can wear is constant sense of *Adab* (Ethics) without any doubt

1090- Through *Adab* only the servant can reach Heaven and accede to the Neighbourhood of the MOST GRACIOUS

1091- So any such that intends to attain GOD's Presence (*Hadratu-l-Lāh*) without it is assuredly an insane person who has not reflected in the least

1092- The Masters assert that sense of *Adab* is nearly the two thirds of devoutness owing to its obvious advantages

1093/94- The Rules of *Adab* may be divided up into two kinds - *according to the Sheikh kindred to the Deymānī tribe*[154] :
> - Outward Ethics (*Adab Zāhir*) that have to be practised with people
> - Inward Ethics (*Adab Bātin*) one must practise vis-à-vis the LORD of the Creation; [it has been said that] inward *Adab* must necessarily come after the first kind

---

[153]The notion of *Adab* implies as well an idea of moral propriety as that of profound reverence and awe towards the LORD. We may translate it by "Islamic ethics" or "proprieties".
[154] Al-Yadāli.

Title 1

Outward Ethics towards our fellow creatures

1095-1103

As regarding the rules of outward *Adab*, we count amongst them:

a- Fine human qualities,

b- Sense of decency,

c- Always using one's right side[155],

d- Never forgetting to say the *Basmalah*[156] before an act,

e- Respecting the proprieties of eating[157],

f- Using often a toothpick, which is strongly recommended by the Holy Prophet- *Peace and Blessings be upon him* - mostly before each prayer,

g- Shaking warmly, with thy two hands, thy fellow Muslim's hand,

---

[155] In Islam, Believers are commanded to accomplish "positive" actions - as eating, greeting, taking an item, wearing shoes, clothes, entering a house and so- with their right hand or side whereas the "negative" actions - toilet washing, blowing one's nose, getting out from a house and so- have to be made with the left side...

[156]"In the Name of GOD, MOST GRACIOUS, MOST MERCIFUL". *Cf.* note 13.

[157]There is not in Islam a definite barrier between the "profane" and the "sacred", all actions are to be performed in the view to please Who allows them to happen and who gives man intelligence and ability to fulfil them- GOD. So as any daily act, eating has also certain proprieties any Muslim has to comply with; such as: washing one's hands, eating with one's right hand, saying *Bismi-Lāh* first and so.

h- Reading often the Qur-ān,

i- Greeting people in a clear and audible voice,

j- Practising generosity[158],

k- Visiting ill persons,

l- Greeting back one's Muslim Brother,

m- Saying "*Alhamdu li-Lāh* " (Praise be to GOD!) when we sneeze,

n- Saying "*Yarahmuka-Lāh*" (May GOD impart thee mercy) to a person who sneezed and who said "*Alhamdu li-Lāh* ",

o- Putting our right palms on our mouths when we yawn[159],

p- Breaking one's fast [the earlier possible] after sunset,

q- Asking for permission before entering someone's room[160],

---

[158] The importance of a virtuous and kind attitude towards our fellow creatures is shown by this *Hadith Qudsi*, on the authority of Abu Mas'ud al-Ansari (may GOD be pleased with him), who said that the Messenger of GOD (may blessings and peace be upon him) said: *"A man from among those who were before you was called to account. Nothing in the way of good was found for him except that he used to have dealings with people and, being well-to-do, he would order his servants to let off the man in straitened circumstances [from repaying his debt]. The Prophet(PBH) said that God said: We are worthier than you of that (of being so generous). Let him off."*

[159] And saying "*A'ūzu bil-Lāhi mina Shaytāni-r-Rajīm.*" (I seek GOD's Protection against Satan, the Damned). One can also use one's left hand but in using the back of one's palm...

[160] Cf. Qur-ān xxiv. 27-29: *"O ye who believe! Enter not houses other than your own, until ye have asked permission and saluted those in them: that is best for you, in order that ye may heed (what is seemly). If ye find no one in the house, enter not until permission is given to you. If ye are asked to go back, go back; that makes for*

r- Forgiving the offender[161],

s- Giving to whom refuses to give thee,

t- Becoming friends again with who has broken off with thee,

u- Being kind with everybody - *waken ye up, o my Brethren!, and conform to this-*

1104- Note that such two principles [(t) and (u)] are compulsory regarding your kin and mostly your parents[162], be they idolaters

1105-

v- Bringing up one's children so that they become upright once having grown up,

1106/07- To these classic rules of *Adab Ẕãhir*, I do add for myself

w- Compassion for youth

x- Respect for the elders

---

greater purity for yourselves: and GOD knows well all that ye do. It is no fault on your part to enter houses not used for living, which serve some (other) use for you."
[161]Indeed Sheikh Aḥmadu Bamba himself gave us a fine model of Pardon and Nobleness inasmuch as he forgave publicly all who set themselves on persecuting him for almost 33 years, in writing: " *I have forgiven to all my enemies for the Holy Face of Whom has driven them away; so never shall I try to avenge myself* ", "*I have forgiven to all my enemies with full pure-heartedness*" (Cf. his poem *Midãdĩ*). Cf. also Qur-ãn xxiv. 22: " *Let them forgive and overlook, do you not wish that GOD should forgive you? For GOD is OFT-FORGIVING, MOST MERCIFUL.*"
[162]Cf. Qur-ãn ii. 83: "*And remember We took a Covenant from the Children of Israel (to this effect): worship none but GOD; treat with kindness your parents and kindred, and orphans and those in need; speak fair to people; be steadfast in prayer; and give zakat, then did ye turn back, except a few among you, and ye backslide (even now).*"

y- Act with thy peer as thou wouldst like him acting with thee
- *indeed there are many other fine attitudes [relating to outward ethics we cannot mention here]*

1108- [It has been related on that matter that] once a father addressed his dearly son and gave him this valuable piece of advice:

1109- *"Be thou steadfast in acquiring fine qualities and in acting sincerely, out of any hypocrisy.*

1110- *[O my son!] Adab! Adab! Adab!*[163] *That means respecting and treating kindly thy father and thy mother,*

1111- *...Thy uncle, thy aunt, thy grand-brother and thy Sheikh - indeed this one [the Sheikh] is worthy of respect and of kindness -*

1112- *And any that is older than thee, honour him, and any that is younger, treat him with compassion and gentleness"*

1113- Here will come to an end the developments concerning outward ethics; let us pass now to those which regard inward *Adab*

---

[163]The aim of this threefold injunction is to stress on the particular importance of Ethics in worship...

Title 2

Inward Ethics towards the MOST HIGH

1114- O Man! know that if ever thou show blatant lack of propriety (*Adab*) vis-à-vis the LORD thou wilt be repulsed and [parted from GOD] by Veils!

1115- Being repulsed from the Threshold of GOD's Sublime Gate and being parted from Him by Veils is the most grievous punishment [a worshipper can experience] indeed

1116/33- [Are considered as signs of unseemliness towards the LORD]:

a- Criticising His Decrees through such conjecturing words as "*If ever things were like this*" or "*Were it not*"or "*If perchance*" and so

b- Disparaging His Essence or any of His Manifestations [even indirectly when, for instance] He causes an event [which suits not thee]

c- The same with the Acts He accomplishes through the Honourable Saints[164]; indeed disparaging these ones, either inwardly or outwardly, is considered as an impropriety [towards GOD *Himself*] - *so do love them all*

d- Reserving the right to choose something else [although GOD already ordered],

e- Speculating on the "appositeness" of an event decreed by the MOST GRACIOUS,

e'- Trying to counter His Decision,

---

[164] Miracles and other Wondrous Secrets entrusted to the Saints by GOD (*Cf.* verses 1386-1432)

f- Confiding one's entire trust in the creatures,

g- Fearing the creatures,

h- Complaining to them [about thy misfortunes] - Turn not towards His creatures out of need or of fear, but betake thyself unto the MOST HIGH LORD

i- Always choosing easy answers and more accommodating interpretations[165] - Know that any GOD-seeker (*murīd*)[166] who gets used to always choosing easy ways in applying the Rules of *Shari'a* shall never succeed [in "finding" GOD]

j- Using licit goods without intending thereby to adore GOD - *Who that provides Favours*

j'- ...Or without aiming thereby to get nearer to Him - O Man! have such an intention whenever thou use His Favours, so wilt thou be granted a Fine Reward

k- One has also to use those goods in order to content oneself thereof and to avoid searching for illicit goods; otherwise that would be blameworthy

l- Sleeping during the day [unless one is absolutely compelled to do so] because of one's having spent all the previous night in adoration, for instance

m- Sleeping [even during the night] unless one is exhausted[167],

---

[165]Lax interpretation of Koranic verses and juridical awards, so that one may cheat with one's conscience and give free rein to one's lust, falsely self-assured to stay within the legal limits...

[166]The shade of meaning of the word *Murīd* is here "spiritual novice", "sufi disciple"...

[167]Because night has to be spent in adoration, unless one has a valid constraint.

n- ...Or during Thursday night[168] - *may GOD make our wishes true*

o- [It is likewise considered as improper, regarding His Mightiness] to say "*This* belongs to me"[169] or "*This* harms me"[170]

p- Complaining continuously about thy hardships,

q- Neglecting to take part in congregational prayers,

r- Lack of reverence and meditation during prayer,

s- Neglecting to pay regular visits to the Virtuous Persons,

t- Misappropriating people's goods by means of Religion[171]

u- Heedlessness as far as night worship is concerned,

---

[168]The night of Thursday to Friday is highly regarded in Islam, the reason why spending it entirely in worship is earnestly recommended.

[169]Because everything *belong* to the LORD and not to the creatures but one has however to acknowledge that such a sense of *Tawḥīd* concerns more the Elite of the Servants... (*Cf.* verses 11-13)

[170]Because only the LORD can really *harm*, not the creatures who just carry out the Divine Decision. This concerns likewise the kind of *Tawḥīd* which deals with the transcendental considerations of *Ḥaqīqa* (Basic and True Realities) and not those of the Law (*Shari'a*), which is charged to take into account "rational" outwardly considerations...

[171]In his work *Jawhar Nafis*, the Sheikh gives these followings particulars concerning such a grave sin (verses146 to 149): " *The worst of the creatures are definitely those who make their fortune through the pretext of religion and who live deliberately thereon. Their bellies shall be, in the Hereafter, as gigantic as castles and towers - without [this image] yielding in the least to legend... Scorpions and snakes will crawl therein, torturing them for aye and not shall they be granted the favour to die at length... When they let out a wind, the fetid smell coming from their intestines shall harm all [their criminal companions] that are held under detention in Hell...*"*Cf.* also Qur-ān ix. 34: "*O ye who believe! There are indeed many among the priests and anchorites, who in falsehood devour the wealth of men and hinder (them) from the way of GOD.*"

1134- Indeed such a negligence will impoverish thee in the Hereafter - *spend not the whole night lying in bed as a dead man!*

1135- But waken thou up resolutely for GOD's Sake once people go bed and fight thou against drowsiness

1136- It is not proper that a clear-minded servant sleeps overnight because such a habit will prevent him from achieving his spiritual objectives

1137- If thou wish to be ranked amongst the Elect, be among those who spend their nights in adoration until dawn[172]

1138- Staying wide-awake all the nights, for the Sole Countenance of the MOST GRACIOUS, will shield man from Hell on the Ultimate Day

1139- O my Brethren! know ye that a single pair of rak'a performed in the dead of night

1140- ...Are more profitable than this entire world and all what is therein - as reported [from the Tradition of the Prophet]; *accustom yourselves to them*

1141- It has been related that the Best of all Messengers - *upon him the Finest* Pair *of Blessings-*

1142- ...Has said that he would have classed such two rak'a amongst the *Faráīd* (Obligatory Acts of worship) were it not their difficult

---

[172]Cf. Qur-ān li. 15-19: "*As to the Righteous, they will be in the midst of Gardens and Springs, taking joy in the things which their LORD gives them, because, before then, they have done good deeds. They were in the habit of sleeping but little by night, and in the hours of early dawn, they (were found) praying for Forgiveness; and in their wealth there is a due share for the beggar and the deprived.*"

performance [for the *common run* of Believers][173] - *indeed this shows how meritorious they are*

1143- Our dear Sheikh Junayd and our Master Ibn-al-Qāsim - *may the LORD of the Worlds be Satisfied with both of them -*

1144- ...Have appeared in a dream - each of them and separately - to some virtuous men who questioned them about their after-death situation

1145- Both of them gave the same answer: "***Nought about my numerous good deeds has availed for my Salvation except the pair of rak'a I was regularly performing at dawn***"

1146- And that, although their both having spent their whole lifetimes in worshipping the MAJESTIC; [alas!] what about others who dissipate their lives in trivialities!

1147- If ever thou prove thyself incapable of praying during the night and of fasting during the day, and if moreover thou persist in sining

1148- ...There is no doubt thou wilt be held in contempt on Doomsday - unless thou repent in stopping *forthwith* [such a thoughtless behaviour] and in regretting it

1149- Whoever gets used to *lengthening* his standing stance while praying in the night, GOD will *shorten* in favour of him the Duration of the Last Day

1150- If thou revive a night in performing *Dhikr*, thou wilt be considered in the morning as pure and sinless as thou wert at thy birth

---

[173]*Cf.* Qur-ān ii. 286: "*On no soul doth GOD place a burden greater than it can bear.*"

1151/52- Now regarding precautions which make it easier to keep awake, we count:

- ❶ Temperance in eating,
- ❷ Avoiding excessive strain [during the day],
- ❸ Wasting not one's time in vain worldly affairs,
- ❹ Eschewing sins

1153- Because sins entail the hardening of the heart and lead man unto   ruin   -
as previously mentioned[174]

1154- Furthermore they intervene between man and his chances to benefit from the Divine Mercy - *may GOD protect us from peril*

1155- Our Noble Sheikh Sufyãn At-<u>Th</u>awrĩ - *may the RULER impart him an excellent Reward and be Satisfied with him* – related us:

1156- *"I happened once to stay unable to wake up in the night and to worship GOD during five consecutive months*

1157- *...Because of one single sin I had committed!"*

1158- Asked about this, he replied: *"I happened to meet a man that was crying [in fear and reverence of GOD]. Then I thought inwardly: '[Pooh!] Some ostentatious fellow."*

1159- And that was enough! Because evil will always entail evil just the way good always brings about good

1160- *Some* quantity of each can cause *much* thereof - thence never consider any offence as negligible[175]

1161- It has been also said that whenever a Muslim misses a congregational prayer it is due to a sin he has committed somehow

---

[174]*Cf.* verse 873.
[175]*Cf.* Qur-ãn xxx. 10: *"In the long run evil will be the end of those who do evil."*

1162- So his involuntary sleep in the night is considered as a punishment proceeding from GOD

1163- Except however - *I do make this reservation* - the sleep of the Combatants of Badr[176] - *may the MOST GRACIOUS be Pleased with them for aye-*

1164- Because their dream was heralding the good tidings of their upturn and the removal of their affliction by GOD

1165- Any sin can prevent the servant from praying in the night - *do give credit to this speech of mine!*

1166-However, the most obvious cause liable to veil the heart so as to prevent the Believer from waking in the night - *according to the Chosen Master* -

1167- ...Is eating illicit food - unlike lawful and *pure* food which makes the heart *purer*

1168- *"How often bad food prevented a servant from waking in the night and led him unto ruin!"*

1169- *"How often a glance [cast over indecencies] prevented man from reading a Sūrah!* ", the Masters wondered

---

[176]This refers to the first Battle fought by the little Muslim Community on Friday, the 17th of Ramaḏān, during the second year of the Hijra. About 150 kilometres south-west of Madinah, in the plain of Badr, the group of exiled Makkan Muslims (*Muhājir*), led by the Holy Prophet - Peace be on him- and assisted by their friends of Madinah (*Anṣār*), defeated the overwhelming force of their Pagan enemies of Makkah, in spite of their being just few Combatants, mostly ill-armed. *Cf.* Qur-ān viii. 11: "*Remember he covered you with drowsiness, to give you calm as from Himself, and He caused rain to descend on you from heaven, to clean you therewith, to remove from you the stain of Satan, to strengthen your hearts, and to plan your feet firmly therewith.*"

1170/73- Now let us mention in verses some practices liable to facilitate night worship:

❶ Listening to Koranic verses and other profitable stories[177] so as to become aware of its Advantages and to have one's hope strengthened,

❷ Preserving the heart from hatred,

❸ Preserving the heart from falsity,

❹ And from overmuch concern for vain worldly affairs - *so may GOD accept our deeds -*

1174- Because once such worldly worries take hold of the heart, man will meditate during his prayer only on what is bothering him

1175- ...Not in the least on his prayer, even if apparently he recites the Qur-ãn - *do refrain from thinking too much over daily problems and beware of lost deeds*

1176- As for the person that is prevented from praying overnight by his irrepressible need for sleeping

1177- He has to perform his *Nawãfil* (supererogatory devotions) after Sunset Prayer (*Maghrib*) and after Night Prayer (*'Ishã*) - *this is well-established*

1178- He must also strive hard to wake before dawn and to leave bed before sunrise

1179- Once awaken he must strive to perform his prayers at the two points of the day[178] - *act thou with steadfastness, o my Brother!*

---

[177]The stories of Godly Men who were assiduous to nocturnal devotions.

[178]Dawn and sunset; so the cycle will go on because that person will have to endeavour again so as to perform the Sunset Prayer (*Maghrib*), to fulfil his devotions after it and so on.

1180- In case he is unable of behaving so - [owing to some other constraint] as illness[179]

1181- ...He must wake during the night and [stay in devotion or in meditation] a short time corresponding to that sufficient to perform four rak'a or to milk an ewe

1182- ...As conveyed from the Tradition of the Messenger - *upon Him the Finest Blessings of Whom has sent Him-*

1183- If ever one is still unable to do so, just two rak'a will suffice

1184- In case [we are so unwell] to manage thereto, we have to sit and to invoke the ETERNAL-ABSOLUTE, the face turned towards the Holy Ka'ba,

1185- ...Meditating (*Fikr*) and uttering His Names (*Dhikr*) during some while - *this is surely far preferable to sprawling stiffly as a buried body!*

1186- Any person who claims to love the LORD and who spends all his nights sleeping however

1187- ... Such a one is assuredly a liar! - as revealed it GOD Himself to the Prophet David - *upon him and upon all his Fellow [Prophets], Peace and Blessings-*

1188/90- [Other bad habits liable to prevent the servant from praying in the night are] - according to the Erudite -
   ❺ Virulent disparagement [of the Virtuous Muslims]

   ❻ Putting forward legal excuses [that are quite untrue, so one may get rid of one's duty]

---

[179]Cf. Qur-ān vii. 42: " *No burden do We place on any soul, but that which it can bear.*"

❼ Too much concern for aestheticism [physical appearance and the like],

❽ Paying court to influential authorities in order to win fame [or wealth],

❾ Claiming falsely lofty spiritual degrees (*Maqāmāt*),

❿ Or even aiming exclusively such *Maqāmāt* through one's night worship[180] - *be thou watchful!*

---

[180]Disregarding so the *Sole* Countenance of the MAJESTIC LORD; this sort of *Tawhīd*- the finest any Muslim must strive to achieve- which dismisses all considerations differing from the Sole Face of the LORD, constitutes that of the Elite of worshippers and the Height of *'Ubudiyyah* (true quality of GOD's Servant)

Man's Four Duties towards
the Majestic Lord 181

1191- Other Duties towards GOD have been set out by the Men of Faith; each of them being closely connected to a particular situation

1192- Mind to behave properly whenever thou art in one of these four situations, for they cannot be retrieved once past

1193/94 ❶ The Duties towards the MAJESTIC of **who that is worshipping** are:
    a- Knowing that all his deeds proceed from GOD's Will

    b- Rendering thanks to GOD (*Shukr*) [for having ranked him among the good-doers]

    c- Worshipping none but Him, in absolute purity (*Ikhlãs*) and out of any self-conceit

    d- [Realising one's shortcomings and soliciting from His Kindness and His Nobleness] to veil them before our peers

1195- If thou succeed in considering GOD's worship through such two *eyes* [*Shukr* and *Ikhlãs*], thou wilt certainly surpass any worshipper that does not so

1196/98- ❷ Now regarding the Duties towards the LORD of **who that is granted Favours and Benefits**, they are:
    a- Acknowledging that it is the MOST HIGH - *Who that guides whomsoever He pleases* - who has imparted such benefits,

    b- Being fully convinced that He is the *Only One* who has granted them,

---

181 As part of *Adab*.

c- Realising that all intermediaries and other rational means are totally subjected to the Will of the CREATOR,

d- However thanking as well the MAJESTIC as people that acted as intermediaries

1199- So wilt thou conform simultaneously to *Haqīqah* and *Shari'a*[182]- *indeed GOD commands to combine both of these*

1200- Any that neglects thanking GOD is guilty of unbelief but whoever disregards thanking the mediators is considered as ungrateful

1201- [Another duty is]
e- Being as well pleased with the *benefits* as with [GOD], the *BENEFACTOR HIMSELF - mind to combine these*[183]

1202- For any benefit originates from His Kindness [and it is known that thinking over delights leads unto loving who that has granted them]

1203- Be not delighted by thy favours only because of their having satisfied thy needs, for such a behaviour may delude thee

1204- [Is likewise considered as a duty]
f- Making use of GOD's Advantages to adore Him better - so wilt thou be honoured once "beyond the veil"

1205- Now, as for GOD's granting benefits to some people whilst these persist in making mischief with

---

[182] See glossary.
[183] *Cf.* Qur-ān xvi.114: "*So eat of the sustenance which GOD has provided for you, lawful and good; and be grateful for the favours of GOD, if it is He Whom ye serve.*"

1206- ...And refuse to thank Him duly; know that such a "paradox" is naught but delusive and transitory well-being, not at all the fulfilment of their wishes! [184]

1207/1210-

❸ Concerning the Duties owed to GOD by a person **who has committed a glaring sin**, they are:

a- Fearing His Grievous Chastisement,

b- Repenting forthwith, without any delay and crying one's heart out[185]

c- Beseeching GOD's Pardon,

d- Imploring Him to give us the Fortitude to stay upright from now forth

---

[184] Indeed it may seem puzzling to a shallow spirit that the wrong-doers are often imparted plenty wealth and honours here below unlike virtuous men who are often deprived of material means... *Primo,* one has to call to one's mind that GOD Himself holds in a highly negligible regard this short life in comparison with the Wonders of the Coming World and, *secundo,* we must know that such favours are nothing but the means by which GOD will increase the punishment promised to the mischievers on Doomsday. *Cf.* Qur-ān ix.85: " *Nor let their wealth nor their children dazzle thee: GOD's Wish is to punish them with these things in this world, and that their souls may depart while they are unbelievers*" *Cf.* also Qur-ān xxviii. 60-61: "*The (material) things which ye are given are but the conveniences of this life and the glitter thereof, but that which is with GOD is better and more enduring: will ye not then be wise? Are (these two) alike? -one to whom We have made a goodly promise, and who is going to reach its (fulfilment), and one to whom We have given the good things of this life, but who, on the Day of Judgment, is to be among those brought up (for punishment)?*" Refer also to the Prophetic Maxim "*This world is a prison for the Believers and a paradise for the unbelievers*"

[185] Tears may indeed seem to be shameful for a "manly man" but that concerns certainly not those shed in fearing the LORD. *Cf.* Qur-ān xvii. 107-109: "*Those who were given knowledge beforehand, when [GOD's Verses] are recited to them, fall down on their faces in humble prostration and say:* 'Glory to our LORD! Truly has the promise of our LORD been fulfilled!' *They fall down on their faces in tears, and it increases their earnest humility*"

e- Thanking however GOD because such a sin could have been more serious and because it has not lead us straight unto definitive ruin,

f- Calling however to one's mind GOD's Infinite Clemency[186]

g- ...And His Unfathomable Subtlety liable to conceal a benefit wherever He pleases[187]

1211- For such an awkward situation can well shield from self-conceit [the servant who was nearly falling into because of his sinlessness]

1212- And there is no doubt that self-conceit is far more dangerous than an unfortunate mistake, because such a vice diverts definitively the servant from the Path towards GOD, the SUPREME JUDGE,

1213- ...And incites him unto deluding self-confidence due to his ignorance [of the True Realities] and due to his heedlessness

1214-- ❹ The Duties towards the LORD for the servant **who is experiencing misfortunes and hardships** are:
    a- Fine forbearance,

b- Keeping hopeful [in the Heavenly Rescue] so one may be praised thereof [in the Hereafter by GOD]

1215- It is not proper that a servant blame the MASTER or show repulsion for one of His Acts, be it an ordeal

---

[186]On which the Muslim must never lose hope. *Cf.* Qur-ān xxxix. 53: "*Say:* " O my Servants who have transgressed against their souls! Despair not of the Mercy of GOD: for GOD forgives all sins: for He is OFT-FORGIVING, MOST MERCIFUL.""

[187]Where human reason cannot grasp it at the outset...

1216- Because [even if thou feel some trouble to realise it fully] know that GOD is more MERCIFUL to the creatures than they may be for their own selves or their own parents may be for them

1217- He ultimately "intends" [through all His Acts and Recommendations] nought but our good[188], the reason for which it is judged highly unfair to blame Him

1218/19-

> c- Beseech thou Him so that He remove thy harm and grant thee [material and spiritual]welfare,

> d- Do feel satisfied of aught He might decide,

> e- Cease not using rational means (asbāb) to the utmost of thy ability[189],

> f- Give up complaining to the creatures about thy misfortunes

---

[188] Verily GOD's Mercy towards mankind is Infinite and Wondrous to any spirit which has been given clear-sightedness... Cf. Qur-ān xvii. 20 "Of the Bounties of thy LORD we bestow freely on all- these as well as those: the Bounties of thy LORD are not closed (to anyone)" " GOD doth wish to make clear to you and to guide you into the ways of those before you; and (He doth wish to) turn to you (in Mercy): and GOD is ALL-KNOWING, ALL-WISE " (iv.26). " Why turn they not to GOD and seek His forgiveness? For GOD is OFT-FORGIVING, MOST MERCIFUL."(v.74) " Say: 'To whom belongeth all that is in the heavens and on earth?' Say: 'To GOD. He hath inscribed for Himself (the rule of) Mercy." (vi.12) " When come to thee those who believe in Our Signs, say: 'Peace be on you'; your LORD has inscribed for Himself (the rule of) Mercy: verily if any of you did evil in ignorance, and thereafter repented, and amended (his conduct), lo! He is OFT-FORGIVING, MOST MERCIFUL"(vi.54) " So say: 'O my LORD! Grant Thou forgiveness and mercy! For Thou art the Best of those who show mercy!'"(xxiii.118) "And He giveth you of all that ye ask for but if ye count the favours of GOD, never will ye be able to number them. Verily, man is given up to injustice and ingratitude." (xiv. 34)

[189]And within the limits permitted by Islamic Law regarding Kasb (Cf. verses 1036-1056)

1220- If ever thou happened to turn toward people and to moan about thy worries [disregarding so their Very LORD], do repent thereof and avoid henceforth such a common reflex

1221- Any calamity which strikes us originates in fact from *our* misdeeds and is naught but the fruit of our *own* sins[190]

1222- Hence it follows that abusing those who have done us *injustices* is itself an *injustice* - as agreed on all the Masters

1223- That is for this same reason the Wise Doctors consider that favours are often hidden into hardships[191]

1224/26-

g- Thank GOD because such a misfortune could have been worst and could have weakened thy very faith

h- Render Him thanks also for His having treated thee as He commonly does with His Noble Friends[192] [in trying thy forbearance] - *so wilt thou find Salvation*

---

[190]*Cf.* Qur-ān xlii. 30:"*Whatever misfortune happens to you, is because of the things your hands have wrought, and for many (a sin) He grants forgiveness*".

[191]*Cf.* Qur-ān xciv. 5:"*So, verily, with every difficulty there is a relief.*" The very life of the Sheikh Ahmadu Bamba has shown the reality of such a Divine Rule because the holy man underwent for about thirty-three years (from 1895 to 1927) the toughest persecutions and injustices from the French colonial authorities. This having not in the least weakened his resolve to lift GOD's Word. At the contrary, he never ceased proclaiming his attachment to the Eternal Truth through all his innumerable writings (more than 10,000 books). "*I am and will stay the subject of GOD and the servant of His Blessed Prophet whenever I may be...*", he never ceased upholding and *practising* (*Cf.* Biography of Sheikh Ahmadu Bamba, www.majalis.org). The Infinite Spiritual Advantages GOD MOST HIGH impart him -as to all that have sincerely taken the oath of fealty to him-, his eminent prestige which led towards him people from all horizons are a few evidences that " the LORD will never suffer the blood shed in His Path to be lost"...

[192]Godly Persons which are called *wālī* (*i. e.* Friends [of GOD])

i- Feel grateful considering that He has chosen to punish thee _now_, in _this_ world, without waiting for the Next One

1227/1228-

[O my Brother!] I advise thee to take this recommendation as a motto:

"Endeavour to permanently asking for GOD's Forgiveness before His Wrath fall on thee. Cease not praising Him and never admit that True Power and Effectual Means might be the prerogative of anyone but the LORD of Bounties!"

Patience

(Sabr) [193]

1229/31- O Brother of mine! Know that [there are different sorts of patience] among which we will mention:

❶ **Patience** [in bearing steadfastly the efforts required by] the adoration of the MOST GRACIOUS - *how LOFTY He is!*

❷ **Patience** in restraining oneself from sinning; mostly at the first blow [of the ordeal or of the temptation] - as put it the Upright One, our Master Muḥammad - *may the ETERNAL-ABSOLUTE grant him Eternal Peace and Blessings, as to his Kindred and his Companions-*

1232- Once the harm already stroke, a behaviour liable to make our patience finer is concealing it to people and in behaving as usual; as if we were in perfect peace

1233/34-
❸ **Patience** in resisting temptations and all forbidden pleasures,

❹ **Patience** in avoiding bad thoughts,

---

[193]As part of *adab*. Regarding the definition of Ṣabr we may read in Yusuf Ali's translation of the Qur-ān (note 61): "*The Arabic word Ṣabr implies many shades of meaning, which it is impossible to comprehend in one English word. It implies (1) patience in the sense of being thorough, not hasty; (2) patient perseverance, constancy, steadfastness, firmness of purpose; (3) systematic as opposed to spasmodic or chance action; (4) a cheerful attitude of resignation and understanding in sorrow, defeat, or suffering, as opposed to murmuring or rebellion, but saved from passivity or listlessness, by the element of constancy or steadfastness.*
"

❺ **Patience** in [practising extreme sobriety or even ceasing definitively from] using delightful food for the Countenance of the MAKER[194]

1235- Moreover it has been noticed that the word s̲abr (patience) may be followed by three prepositions [implying three different situations during which the servant has to keep patience] - *whoever succeeds in practising it in each of these cases will deserve the Divine Love indeed*

1236- The first preposition is "while", the second is "notwithstanding " and the last one is "in"

1237- Concerning the first kind, that is patience *while* adoring GOD or *while* experiencing adversities - *this is indeed among the finest attitudes one may adopt*

1238- Our LORD will raise more any that is endowed with such a virtue to three hundred (300) Degrees

---

[194]This kind of patience is indeed practised by those who have attained the highest degree of S̲abr. The Sheikh himself, since his younger days, took the habit to strive in such a sublime self-restraint, and we may find thereof an example in the book he devoted to the narration of the main events of his eight-years' exile. This happened after his five-years' stay in the forest of Mayumba (Gabon, Central Africa): " *Just after my departure from Mayumba island, I deliberately gave up many things among which certain whose use is quite lawful [in the view of the Islamic Legislation (Shari'a)], for GOD's Noble Face in return for [the Favours] that are with Him. I made that 'bargain' at a Price that will last as well here below as in the Hereafter and that will never be withdrawn from me, and that will never fade away. I will mention here, among such things I 'traded', just few of them. That is through such a Covenant I became the friend of GOD MOST HIGH and that of His Messenger -upon him, his Kindred and his Companions GOD's Blessings. Among those things I laid down is the use of the sugar provided [as a ration] by French Authorities. [GOD], That in Whose Love I am entirely drowned imparted me the most blissful Delights in return for such abstinences. Amongst those things I renounced [for the Holy Face] was the eating of a fruit growing on that island and that was yet more delicious than many other varieties of fruits (...)*" (in his book called "Jazāu-s-Shakūr " (The Tribute Paid to [GOD], Who that desserveth Thanks), p.29)

1239- Then comes patience _notwithstanding_ worldly pleasures, _notwithstanding_ bad thoughts and aught that is forbidden, for the Sole Sake of GOD, Who that grants Peace

1240- Whoever strives in such a kind of patience will be raised to six hundred (600) Degrees by GOD

1241- [The last kind of patience is] patience _in_ times of peace and happiness; this is assuredly the hardest and the most meritorious of them all

1242- Because our LORD will raise [the wealthy person that forbears from forgetting heavenly purposes] to nine hundred (900) Degrees

1243- Indeed only who that believes firmly in the future Reward [imparted to the patient servants] will stand patient _while_ experiencing hardships

1244- Likewise man will never bear patience _in_ times of peace unless he gives due credit to the Future Life [and its Tremendous Features][195]

1245- The most deserving and brave person is indeed who that manages to remain patient _in_ times of peace and joy

1246- Such patience consists in not confiding in one's material welfare, in not letting oneself deluded by one's material goods

1247- ...And in not giving oneself up to their joys with sensual pleasure and constant exultation - _indeed such thoughtlessness exposes man to terrible Trials_[196]

---

[195] Cf. Qur-ān ii. 45-46: "_Seek [GOD's] Help with patient perseverance and prayer: it is indeed hard, except to those who are humble, who bear in mind the certainty that they are to meet their LORD, and that they are to return to Him_ "

[196]Cf. Qur-ān x. 21: "_When We make mankind taste of some mercy after adversity hath touched them, behold! they take to plotting against Our Signs! Say: "Swifter to plan is GOD!"_ _Verily, Our messengers record all the plots that ye make!_" and Qur-

1248- This kind of patience consists also in not throwing oneself into sport and pleasures due to one's lacking of useful purpose in life[197]

1249- It consists in not devoting oneself to lust and voluptuousness, and in regularly discharging the financial duties [imposed by Islamic Law (*Shari'a*) and Love for GOD] - *any that behaves so will, of a surety, gain profit*

1250- Fine forbearance implies also imprisoning the Soul in the "cells" of hunger[198] so as to prompt her to seek for GOD's Light and to restrain from showing "bad manners"[199] vis-à-vis the LORD of the Throne

1251- It implies to always abide by the rules of fine *Adab* (Ethics) with the MOST HIGH

1252- One has also to remain patient in facing expenses on GOD's Path, out of any fear of poverty

1253- In giving to any rightful claimant all their rights for the Holy Face

1254- In supporting one's family and in bearing serenely harm stemming from their acts and words

1255- Because our kin stand for the "path" which can lead us unto the MAJESTIC LORD; o my Friend! know that the *least* we are compelled to do in their favour is caring about them

---

ān xiii. 26: " *(The worldly) rejoice in the life of this world. But the life of this world is little comfort compared to the Hereafter.*"

[197]Cf. Qur-ān lxiv. 15: "*Your riches and your children may be but a trial: whereas GOD, with him is the highest Reward.*" Qur-ān vii. 51: "*Such as took their religion to be mere amusement and play, and were deceived by the life of the world. That day shall We forget them as they forgot the meeting of this day of theirs, and as they were wont to reject Our signs.*"

[198] See also verses 914 to 917

[199]Lack of *adab*

1256- The *highest* degree [of patience with our family] consists in feeling satisfied[200] by the LORD having entrusted us such a burden and in always confiding in Him as far as their means of living are concerned

1257- The *medium* degree is meeting stoically one's household expenses, feeling compassion for them

1258- ...And resigning oneself to their demands without yielding to any bad influence

1259- Another feature of fine patience is the worshipper's stamina in withstanding temptations to accomplish miracles [before people] or to talk about the wondrous mysteries GOD might have unveiled to him through *Kashf*[201]

1260- Patience also implies restraining oneself from loving public thanking

1261- ...And from liking for leadership and praises, in striving to perform discreetly and humbly one's good deeds

1262- Being patient means also staying in constant humility as a sign of preference for the Wondrous and Eternal Future World to this vile and negligible present world[202]

1263- ...So as to get closer to the LORD thereby – *He that Satisfies any need outside of the creatures*

---

[200]Cf. Qur-ān lxx. 5: "*Therefore do thou hold Patience, a Patience of beautiful (contentment).*"

[201] *Kashf* is the unveiling of hidden Realities and Mysteries attained by the Saint through long time of worship during which he succeeded- with GOD's Help- to purify his heart from all falsities and stains which were covering the "mirror of his heart" so as to prevent the Divine Light to be reflected thereon.

[202]Cf. Qur-ān xciii. 4: "*And verily the Hereafter will be better for thee than the present.*"; xxxv. 5: "*O men! Certainly the promise of GOD is true, let not then this present life deceive you, nor let the Chief Deceiver deceive you about GOD.*"

1264- In order also to achieve the virtues relating to the state of *'Ubudiyyah* [the quality of authentic servant][203]

1265- Such Virtues which enable man to be raised to high Degrees and which incite him to no longer rebelling against the SUBLIME KING

1266- Patience must also prompt thee unto concealing thy good deeds and unto subduing thy Soul

1267- In depriving her of succulent fruits, be they quite licit - *waken thou!*

1268- Patience implies also the concealment of thy kindnesses and thy discretion in giving alms - *never cease acting with disinterestedness* [204]

1269- It has been said that the virtue of concealing one's pains and adversities [205], as the habit of hiding one's alms

1270- ...Are the most precious Treasure one may keep back before GOD [for the Coming World]

1271- Behaving with so much dignity that people could not guess about our poverty is most praiseworthy but that is indeed one of the hardest thing man can manage in

---

[203]State we are tempted to translate by "Servantness". It consists in a state of true subjection toward the LORD which implies keen knowledge of His Absolute Kingship (*Rubūbiyyah*). That is indeed the best state of mind a worshipper may attain...

[204]Cf. Qur-ān xcii. 18-21: *"Those who spend their wealth for increase in self-purification, and have in their minds no favour from anyone for which a reward is expected in return, but only the desire to seek for the Countenance of their LORD MOST HIGH; and soon will they attain (complete) satisfaction."*

[205]In bearing them stoically and in imploring GOD MOST HIGH for their removal.

1272- However the highest stage of patience consists [for the true devotees] in keeping perfectly patient during *Mujālasah* sessions with GOD[206]

1273- ...In "listening" attentively to Him, in concentrating fully one's attention and interest in Him while alternating between a state of fear and that of hope

1274- Patience in Loving GOD, in fostering one's sense of shame and of propriety towards Him[207] [is also highly valued]

1275- As for patience in taking delight *from* His Decisions, that is keeping composed whatever His Decree might be, be it "for better or for worse"

1276- ...And being convinced that such an Act is a benefit one may use to get nearer to the LORD

1277- ...And that it proceeds from His Infinite Wisdom which tries man thereby

1278- Know also that perfect patience involves many Advantages before the MAJESTIC

1279- We may count amongst them Salvation and the granting of our wishes here below and in the Hereafter out of any jeopardy

1280- Patience will grant Tomorrow lofty degrees [in the Garden of Bliss] and permits to triumph over one's enemies in this world - *mind to bear patience, o ye disciples!*

---

[206]Session of prayers and invocations during which the Mystic lives in the Divine *Presence*.

[207]The word *ḥayā* implies an idea of shame for one's failings before GOD, the ALL-KNOWING, and that of a proper behaviour vis-à-vis the LORD owing to one's gratefulness (*Shukr*) for His having veiled kindly such failings to our peers...

1281- Patience takes man unto leadership and unto guiding his fellow creatures, it permits also to win honour and to achieve our LORD's Praising

1282- That drives us unto loving GOD and grants eternal Rewards to any that devotes himself thereto

1283- That imparts Happiness, GOD's Blessings, Mercy and Salvation, here below as in the Beyond

1284- The Prophet - *Peace and Blessings be upon his Holy Person* - said in a *hadīth*: **"To whomever the LORD of the Creation Wishes well, He maketh him undergo hardships."**

1285- ... So as to give him the opportunity to win the great amount of Rewards relating to the forbearance of such hardships - *bear thou then patience*

1286- It has been also asserted [still in the *Hadīth*] that: **"No harm strikes a Believer - be it a "nasab" or a "wasab", whatever anguish or pain**

1287- **...Or even the sting of a throbbing little thorn - unless GOD intends [through such a harm] to rid him of some sin he had committed."**

1288- The clear-sighted Masters have construed the word *nasab* as: fatigue, strain

1289- And the word *wasab* as "illness" - this *hadīth* has been simultaneously reported by the two Sheikhs [Al-Bukhārī and Muslim][208],

---

[208]Bukhāri (d. 870) and Muslim (d. 874): the two most accredited reporters of Prophetic maxims (*ahadīth*); their authoritative books are called the *Sahīh* (The Authentic Reports).

1290- Who have taken it from Abū Sa'īd and Abū Hurayrah, who were both Companions of the Prophet - *may the MOST GRACIOUS be satisfied with them-*

1291- It has been said that GOD tries His servants according to their faiths[209]

1292- If He finds thee firm and patient, He will stiffens thy trials [until thy sins be totally atoned for]; but in case He finds thee overwhelmed or in despair, He will either cease trying thee or relieve thy pain[210]

1293- So the patient servant will never get out of his hardships until he is totally cleansed of any kind of sins he committed

1294- Indeed any one who spends undisturbed and perfectly peaceful life in this world will deeply regret it in the Next World, in seeing those who have undergone ordeals

1295- Then he will wish almost he had his body permanently torn into shreds in his past life

1296- ...Because of the Wondrous and Boundless Rewards which will be imparted to the suffering Believers on that Day

1297- [Thus we can understand more why] the LORD often overburdens His believing and striving Servants with misfortunes on this earth[211]

---

[209]Cf. Qur-ān xxix. 2-3: *"Do men think that they will be left alone on saying, "We believe", and that they will not be tested? We did test those before them, and GOD will certainly know those who are true from those who are false."*

[210] ...So much so that thou wilt remain weighed down with sins or be deprived of many Rewards.

[211]Cf. Qur-ān ii. 153: *"O ye who believe! Seek help with patient perseverance and prayer: for GOD is with those who patiently persevere."* Qur-ān iii. 200: *"O ye who believe! Persevere in patience and constancy; vie in such perseverance; strengthen each other and fear GOD that ye may prosper."* Qur-ān xi. 115: *"And be steadfast in patience; for verily GOD will not suffer the reward of the righteous to perish."*

1298- "Just the way a caring father looks after his children"

1299- Another _hadīth_ [supplements the above-mentioned in saying]: *"GOD will try any of His servant He really Loves with many troubles;*

1300- *If that servant bears patience, He will rank him amongst the Elect. If, moreover, the servant shows satisfaction [of being tried by His MASTER], the LORD will raise him more and will rank him amongst the Chosen* Par Excellence"

1301- In the Hereafter, the hapless righteous will neither be submitted to [the deeds weighing] on the Scales nor will [their actions be thoroughly examined] through personal Records[212]

1302- Nay, but their Rewards will be merely heaped up as mountains before them Tomorrow[213] - *Bliss to them!*

1303- [So do hold to this advice of mine]: "Praise thou GOD during times of *good fortune* and do bear patience during times of *misfortune*"

1304- There were among the Virtuous Ancients certain who became sad if ever they stayed peacefully a certain time without experiencing any kind of trial

1305- And if ever they remained a whole year without undergoing any sort of hardship

1306- ...Concerning their wealth, their progenies or their own persons, they became deeply afflicted thereof

---

[212]Books of Deeds which will be placed before every Soul and that will leave out nothing, be it small or great...

[213]Cf. Qur-ān xvi. 41-42: *"To those who leave their homes in the cause of GOD, after suffering oppression, we will assuredly give a goodly home in this world; but truly the reward of the Hereafter will be greater. If they only realised (this)! (They are) those who persevere in patience, and put their trust on their LORD."*

1307- ...Owing to the great hopes [about the Future Life] their LORD's trials were arousing in them - *there is no doubt that such men were People of High Wisdom!*[214]

1308- A true Believer stays never forty days without feeling any fear,

1309- Either by a very frightening prospect or by some other trial likely to increase his afterlife Rewarding

1310/14- Amongst the numerous sorts of liquid there are certain which will be converted into Priceless Treasures once before the MOST GRACIOUS: two kinds of *drop* and two kinds of *mouthful*
❶ A drop of **tear** shed in the dead of night by a striving worshipper who prostrates [in humility and awe for GOD]

❷ A drop of **blood** shed during an effort[215] intended to [give victory] and to raise GOD's Word

❸ A bitter "mouthful of **anger**" man stifles in hiding his pain and in remaining good-hearted so as to obtain the Satisfaction of the ETERNAL-ABSOLUTE

❹ A "mouthful of **affliction**" choked back in bearing patiently adversity- *be steadfast in patience, o my Brother!, so wilt thou gain Guidance*

---

[214]*Cf.* Qur-ān ii. 155: "*Be sure We shall test you with something of fear and hunger, some loss in goods, lives and the fruits (of your toil), but give glad tiding to those who patiently persevere.*" See also Qur-ān iii. 186: "*Ye shall certainly be tried and tested in your possessions and in yourselves; and ye shall certainly hear much that will grieve you, from those who received the Book before you and from those who worship partners besides GOD. But if ye persevere patiently, and guard against evil, -then that indeed is a matter of great resolution.*" and Qur-ān xlvii. 31: "*And We shall try you until We test those among you who strive their utmost and persevere in patience, and We shall try your reported (mettle).*"
[215]We have construed here the word *Jihād* (Holy War) by its widest meaning which is "an effort" [made in GOD's Path]...

1315- [Another significant feature of perfect patience] consists in praying GOD to give us the fortitude to always behave as a true servant, in showing plainly our weakness and our impotence to Him

1316- ...Without aiming thereby any specific Favour - lest one should be rebuked by the LORD, *He who grants Favours*

1317- Because, as regards Himself, He does aught *He* pleases, not what pleases *thee*, o GOD-seeker!

1318- Thus patience is called "the Core of adoration" because of its great value[216] - *mind thou to hold it in high regard*

---

[216]*Cf*. Qur-ān ii. 177: "*It is not righteousness that ye turn your faces towards East or West; but it is righteousness to believe in GOD and the Last Day, and the Angels, and the Book, and the Messengers, to spend of your substance, out of love for Him, for your kin, for orphans, for the needy, for the wayfarer, for those who ask and for the ransom of slaves; to be steadfast in prayer, and give zakat, to fulfil the contracts which ye have made; and* **to be firm and patient***, in pain (or suffering) and adversity, and throughout all periods of panic. Such are the people of truth, the GOD-fearing.*"

Gratefulness towards GOD

(Shukr) [217]

[Its features]

1363/65- True gratefulness to GOD consists in:

❶ Testifying that all benefits proceed from the MAJESTIC LORD[218],

❷ Using such benefits, openly and secretly, for [lawful purposes] which entail GOD's Satisfaction

❸ Feeling humble [before His Grandeur] and modest [before the needy],

❹ ...While showing pride before an arrogant wealthy person,

❺ Devoting exclusively one's deeds to [GOD] to Whom belong every being

1367- Know that *Shukr* is made up with three kinds; each of them leading to corresponding degrees:

---

[217]As part of *Adab.*

[218]Cf. Qur-ān xvi.53-54: "*And ye have no good things but is from GOD: and moreover, when ye are touched by distress, unto Him ye cry with groans. Yet, when He removes the distress from you, behold! some of you turn to other gods to join with their LORD.*" Qur-ān vii. 10: "*It is We Who have placed you with authority on earth, and provided you therein with means for the fulfilment of your life: small are the thanks that ye give!*" Qur-ān xiv. 7-8: "*And remember! Your LORD caused to be declared (publicly):* "*If ye are grateful, I will add more (favours) unto you; but if you show ingratitude, truly My Punishment is terrible indeed.*" *And Moses said:*" *If ye show ingratitude, ye and all on earth together, -yet is GOD Free of all wants, worthy of all praise.*"

- The higher degree
- The medium degree
- The lower degree

1368- The higher degree of gratitude consists in worshipping GOD in the sole order to magnify His Greatness; the medium degree consists in worshipping Him to just comply with His Orders

1369- The lower degree of *Shukr* is worshipping GOD and aiming thereby [not exclusively His Holy Face] but some other purpose [even praiseworthy], as the Rewarding of the Garden of Bliss or Salvation from Chastisement

1370- [As for the other features of real gratitude, they are]

❻ Knowing that well-founded hope consists in feeling hopeful, [while relying in GOD (*Tawakkul*)], using *in the same time* normal and rational means (*Kasb*)[219] and performing good deeds

1371- As for who that gives up any kind of normal means and who hopes however to achieve his aim, such a one may surely be labelled as a thoughtless and unsound person!

1372- His hope is naught but daydream! There is no doubt that his laziness will led him unto ruin

1373/79-

❼ Feeling fearful and taciturn because of the uncertainty about one's real fate,

❽ Absolute sincerity while acting,

❾ Feeling satisfied as well by the *benefits* themselves as the *BENEFACTOR* HIMSELF,

---

[219]*Cf.* verses 1036-1056.

❶⓿ Confiding entirely one's affairs in GOD - *never disregard these, o my Fellow!*

❶⓿ Contemplating GOD [through His countless Manifestations],

❶❷ Giving permanently heed to the LORD,

❶❸ Contenting oneself with the Assistance and the Perfect Knowledge of the LORD of Volition,

❶❹ "Polishing" and keeping pure one's faith with the "Waters" of Repentance,

❶❺ Consuming only licit goods,

❶❻ [O Man!] Do water thy "garden" with showers of devotions and [manure it] with good deeds

❶❼ Regular performance of *Duḥā* prayer[220] ,

❶❽ Regretting past times lost outside worshipping the BENEFACTOR,

❶❾ Eschewing any cause liable to entail woeful end,

1380- *We seek refuge in the MOST GRACIOUS from an inauspicious end, in the name of the Holy Prophet Aḥmad, the Overlord of humankind*

1381- *Upon him, and upon his Eminent Kindred and Noble Companions, finest Peace and Blessings*

1382- [Among such causes of ruin one has to eschew and from which we ask for GOD's Protection, we count]:

---

[220]Supererogatory prayer of two rak'as which has to be accomplished everyday between complete sunrise and noon.

a- Love for this vile world which takes entirely possession of man's heart

1383- ...And which throws him irremediably unto its nugatory affairs, in driving him unto devoting all his aspirations thereto,

1384- ...Unto amassing thoughtlessly goods and unto miserliness and which makes the heart constantly engrossed in seeking for wealth[221]

1385-

    b- Man's persistency in sinning, in blameworthy practices (*bid'ā*), in hypocrisy and vices

---

[221]*Cf.* Qur-ān iii. 180: "*And let not those who covetously withhold of the gifts which GOD hath given them of His Grace, think that it is good for them. Nay it will be the worse for them: soon it will be tied to their necks like a twisted collar, on the Day of Judgment.*"

About the Saints

and their disparagement

1386- [Are likewise held as major causes of damnation] - *listen thou carefully to what I am saying -*

    c- The fact of disparaging the Privileges granted to the Saints

1387- ...In rejecting their declarations about the marvellous Secrets GOD has entrusted to them[222]

---

[222] The question of the outstanding gifts imparted to the Saintly Men has always been the core point of the conflict between supporters and opponents of *Tasawwuf*. These latter hold "*Sūfis*' claims" as heretical and as a grave evidence of *shirk* (giving partners to GOD). Such a controversy has been subject to an interesting examination in The Reliance of the Traveller of the Sheikh Ahmad ibn Naqib al-Misri (p. 1015): " *Question: Have we to considered as an unbeliever someone who says* "A believer knows the Unseen (*al-ghayb*) " *because of GOD MOST HIGH having said:* "No one in the heavens or earth knows the Unseen except GOD " (xxvii. 65) *and* "[He is] the Knower of the Unseen, and discloses not His Unseen to any one" (lxxii. 26)? *(Answer:)* "*He is not unconditionally considered an unbeliever, because of the possibility of otherwise construing his words, for it is obligatory to ask to whomever says something interpretable as either being or not being unbelief for further clarification...If asked to explain and such a person answers:* "By saying "**A believer knows the Unseen**", I meant that GOD could impart certain details of the Unseen to some of the friends of GOD (awliya')" - *this is accepted from him, since it is something logically possible and its occurrence has been documented, being among the countless miracles* (Karāmat) *that have taken place over the ages. The possibility of such knowledge is amply attested by what the Qur-ān inform us about Khidr (xviii. 60-82), and the account related of Abu Bakr Siddiq that he told of his wife being pregnant with a boy, and thus it proved; so of 'Umar who miraculously perceived [note: the Muslim commander Sariya and his army who were in Persia, and while on the pulpit in Madinah giving the Friday sermon, he said ' O Sariya, the mountain!'] warning them of the enemy ambush intending to exterminate the Muslims. Or the rigorously authenticated (Sahih) hadith that the Prophet (PBH) said of 'Umar:* 'He is of those who are spoken to [i.e. pre-naturally inspired].' *What we have mentioned about the Koranic verse [on the unseen] has been explicitly stated by Nawawi in his* Fatawa *where he says:* "It means that no one except God

1388- For my part, I do assert that none denigrates them but a perfect ignoramus or a person devoured by jealousy though his being initiated

1389- Indeed how can one condemn a servant who has turned aside from the creatures with self-restraint so as to worship better his LORD!?

1390- What! How can ye come to run down who that fears duly GOD [as He ordered][223] and that has immolated all his desires [on the altar of Divine Love]?

---

knows this independently and with full cognisance of all things knowable. As for [knowledge imparted through] inimitable prophetic miracles (*mu'jizāt*) and divine favours (*karāmat*) it is through God's giving them to know it that it is known; as it is also the case with what is known through ordinary means." *God MOST GLORIOUS is the ALL-KNOWER of things unseen and their inmost secrets, with primal, intrinsic, supernatural knowledge whose basis no one else has a share in. If any besides HIM has awareness or knowledge, it is their being made aware or given knowledge by HIM - Magnificent and Exalted. They are unable - being servants without capacity - to transcend their sphere or go beyond their limit to draw aside the veils from things unseen, and if not for His pouring something of the knowledge of these things upon their hearts, they would know nothing of it, little or much. Yet this knowledge is disparate in degree, and some of it higher than other of it and more certainly established....The miraculous perceptions* (kashf) *of the Friends of GOD* (awliya') *are a truth we do not deny, for Bukhari relates in his* Sahih *from Abu Hurayrah that the Prophet (PBH) said:* "In the nations before you were people who were spoken to [i.e.: inspired] though they were not prophets. If there is anyone in my Community, it is 'Umar ibn Khattab"

[223]Cf. Qur-ān iii. 102: "*O ye who believe! Fear GOD as He should be feared*". We may find a definition of the word *taqwā* ("fear") as it must be understood in this verse, in Yusuf Ali's commentary (note 427): "*Fear is of many kinds: (1) the abject fear of the coward; (2) the fear of a child or an inexperienced person in the face of an unknown danger; (3) the fear of a reasonable man who wishes to avoid harm to himself or to people whom he wishes to protect; (4) the reverence which is akin to love, for it fears to do anything which is not pleasing to the object of love. The first is unworthy of man; the second is necessary for one immature; the third is a manly precaution against evil as long as it is unconquered; and the fourth is the seed-bed of*

1391- How can ye despise who that is elected by the MAJESTIC LORD of Mankind and whose affairs GOD has taken upon Himself to take *particularly* care of?

1392- [Alas! art thou not aware - *o ignoramus!* - of their Favours?]; GOD shields, by His Mercy, His Saintly Friends from Satan and from any cause of scare and sorrow

1393- He gives them fortitude to master their Lust so much so she has no hold over them; thereby are they safeguarded from delusions[224]

1394- GOD unveils to them His Unfathomable Secrets and other kinds of wondrous knowledge

1395- If ever their impenetrable speech disconcert thee - *o thou layman!* - content thyself with these words of the wise 'Abdu-l-Wadūd:

1396- *"As myself I cannot comprehend the speech of the Saints for I am just* **who I am** *whereas themselves are* **who they are**"

---

righteousness. Those mature in faith cultivate the fourth: at earlier stages, the third or the second may be necessary; they are fear, but not the fear of GOD. The first is a feeling of which anyone should be ashamed." Indeed fear of GOD (*taqwā*) is the core virtue of Muslim practice and the most exalted quality on which the ALMIGHTY lay continuously stress in the Glorious Qur-ān. Thus does it embodies the "soul" of religion, the nucleus without which worship would be void and hollow cytoplasm...

[224] Let us quote the following hadith *qudsi* (revelations which appear not in the Book) reported by Bukhari: "The Prophet said: *"GOD MOST HIGH says:* "He who is hostile to a friend of Mine (*wali*) I declare war against. My Slave approaches Me with nothing more beloved to Me than what I have made obligatory for him, and My Slave keeps drawing near to Me with voluntary works until I love him. And when I love him, I am his hearing with which he hears, his sight with which he sees, his hand with which he seizes, and his foot with which he walks. If he asks Me, I will surely give to him, and if he seeks refuge in Me, I will surely protect him". " *Cf.* also Qur-ān x. 62-63: *"Behold! Verily on the friends of GOD there is no fear, nor shall they grieve: those who believe and (constantly) guard against evil"*

1397- Some of them may fulfil sometimes an act which seems to be outwardly in contradiction with Islamic Law (*Shari'a*); the reason for which the masses often censure them [whereas there is always a sound ground - were it hidden - to the attitude of the *walī*²²⁵]

---

²²⁵ This concerns Saintly persons whose acts and speech appear unlawful according to positive Law (*Shari'a*) though their being quite justified according to Higher Standards of *Haqīqah* (deeper and true realities). Indeed such a question has always divided pros and cons *Tasawwuf*. Let us rehearse here the famous story of Moses and Khidr as related in the Qur-ān (xviii. 64-82) which gives undeniable ground to the assertions of the *Sūfīs*: "...*So [Moses and his attendant] went back on their footsteps, following (the path they had come). So they found one of Our servants on whom We had bestowed Mercy from Ourselves and whom We had taught knowledge from Our own Presence. Moses said to him:* 'May I follow thee, on the footing that thou teach me something of the (Higher) Truth which thou hast been taught?' *(The other) said:* 'Verily thou wilt not be able to have patience with me! For how canst thou have patience about things which are beyond thy knowledge?' *Moses said:* 'Thou wilt find me, if GOD so will, (truly) patient: nor shall I disobey thee in aught.' *The other said:* 'If then thou wouldst follow me, ask me no questions about anything until myself speak to thee concerning it.' *So they both proceeded: until when they were in the boat, he scuttled it. Said Moses:* 'Hast thou scuttled it in order to drown those in it? Truly a strange thing hast thou done!' *He answered:* 'Did I not tell thee that thou canst have no patience with me?' *Moses said:* 'Rebuke me not for forgetting, nor grieve me by raising difficulties in my case.' *Then they proceeded: until when they met a young boy, he slew him. Moses said:* 'Hast thou slain an innocent person who had slain none? Truly a foul (unheard-of) thing hast thou done!' *He answered:* 'Did I not tell thee that thou canst have no patience with me?' *(Moses) said:* 'If ever I ask thee about anything after this, keep me not in thy company: then wouldst thou have received (full) excuse from my side.' *Then they proceeded: until, when they came to the inhabitants of a town, they asked them for food, but they refused them hospitality. They found there a wall on the point of falling down, but he set it up straight. (Moses) said:* 'If thou hadst wished, surely thou couldst have exacted some recompense for it!' *He answered:* 'This is the parting between me and thee: now will I tell thee the interpretation of (those things) over which thou wast unable to hold patience. As for the boat, it belonged to certain men in dire want: they plied on the water. I but wished to render it unserviceable, for there was after them a certain king who seized on every boat by force. As for the youth, his parents were people of faith, and we feared that he would*

1398- The Eminent Master Muḥammadu-l-Ghalāwī - *may the BOUNTIFUL LORD bestow plentifully His Favours on him* - said:

1399- *"Any that criticises the poems of the Saints from a grammatical or prosodic view point is assuredly subject to a trial"*

1400 - Having faith in them is itself a proof of saintliness but disparaging them constitutes an offence

---

grieve them by obstinate rebellion, and ingratitude (to GOD). So we desired that their LORD would give them in exchange (a son) better in purity (of conduct) and closer in affection. As for the wall, it belonged to two youths, orphans, in the Town; there was, beneath it, a buried treasure, to which they were entitled; their father had been a righteous man. So thy LORD desired that they should attain their age of full strength and get out their treasure -a mercy (and favour) from thy LORD. I did it not of my own accord. Such is the interpretation of (those things) over which thou wast unable to hold patience.' "

One of the main teaching of this story on which the *Taṣawwuf*-side lay stress is the evidence of the existence of a kind of wondrous knowledge GOD MOST HIGH reveals to just few chosen people -the Elite of *'Ārifīn* (True Knowers). Another teaching -not the least one- one may draw therefrom is that sometimes the deeper realities originating the rules of *Ḥaqiqāh* (Esoteric Law) can be at a certain variance with that of the Positive Legislation (*Shari'a*); the reason why the acts of the True Godly Men, who have truly attained such a degree (not heretics or blameworthy hypocrites however), have not to be disparaged by the uninitiated. Hence do the *Ṣūfī* Congregation infer the superiority of the Science of *Ḥaqīqah* over that of the formal law, even if both are fundamentally complementary because aiming at the same purpose: the Adoration of the LORD. There are indeed a host of other teachings one can draw from that story such as, for instance, the fifteen rules governing the relationship between a Shaykh and his disciple, as detailed by the Emir Abd-el-Kader in the *Kitābu-l-Mawāqīf* (p.83-89).

1401- The story of the disciple of our Sheikh [Sīdi Mu<u>kh</u>tār Kuntiyu] narrated in his work "The Shield of the GOD-seeker ", is a sufficient evidence thereon[226]

1402- Any who really likes to know the merit and the importance of the Saints before the MASTER of the Throne

1403- ...Let him follow in their footpath [as described] in the work entitled "The Source of Lights in Defending the Dignity of the Saints",

1404- Written by Sīdi Mu<u>kh</u>tār, the Sheikh endowed with Fine Secrets - *may GOD, the MAKER, be Satisfied with him* -

1405- *"Indeed it is harder to recognise a Saintly man than to recognise GOD HIMSELF"*

1406- For GOD's Perfection is obvious [through His Manifestations and countless Signs in the universe], His Greatness is not hidden to any spirit that bothers to meditate deeply thereon

1407- Whereas the Saint Man [as distinguished as he may be] is hiding among his fellow creatures

1408- Eating and drinking with people, he is physiologically subject to the same needs and is affected by evil, like them

1409- His Saintliness is so covered under GOD's Veils than none can recognise him but one of his peers

1410/1411- Each of them has two kinds of Lights - as explained it the True Knowers (*'Ārifīn*) -

---

[226](?) We haven't yet the opportunity to find this book and others old books mentionned by the Sheikh. However we are planning to collect them through Senegal and Mauritania.

❶ A Light of *attraction* which draws towards them any person GOD grants mercy

❷ A Light of *repulsion* which drives off them any damned person

1412- Whoever gives them credit during their various spiritual states will benefit from GOD's Favours

1413- Disparaging them will entail naught but ruin and curse - *do beware of these verses of mine*

1414- Know that the degrees and the behaviours of the Saints are as different as those of the Prophets

1415- There are some amongst them who never accomplish miracles although their having reached the Height of Saintliness

1416- Some others display openly miracles without having attained perfect uprightness however

1417- Certain Saints can fly into the skies or walk on the water[227]

---

[227] It is really paradoxical to some extents that certain "Believers" have come to denigrate harshly the reality of the miraculous acts of the Saints (due most certainly to the influences of certain intellectualist *courants de pensée* which threatens Faith itself) in spite of the Holy Scriptures having related many miracles which occurred in the lives of persons who were not yet Prophets or Messengers. Let us recall the Word of GOD towards Maryam (who is not a Prophet, by scholarly consensus) "*Shake the trunk of the palm tree towards you, and it will let fall fresh ripe dates upon you* " (Qur-ān xix. 25); "*Every time, Zakariyya entered the sanctuary he found provision with her. He said 'O Maryam from whence has this come to you? "And she said* "It is from God" (Qur-ān iii. 37). We may also refer to the miraculous events that took place in the story of the people of the cave (Qur-ān xviii) who, by scholarly consensus, were not Prophets. Vesides there are many authentic *a-hadith* which demonstrated the reality of miracles. The hadith of the three people who took shelter in a cave and when a great stone scaled off its entrance, each in turn made

1418- There are some who can talk with the trees or with the stones

1419- Some *Walīs* can rescue their disciple from danger while this one is afar

1420- Others are capable of averting jeopardy only if who that is calling [in their names] is near them

1421- But any disciple that is calling for help, in case he is keenly attached to the Saint he is turning to

1422- ...And cherishes a true hope in him, the MAJESTIC LORD will improve his lot [out of regard for his Sheikh]

1423- Certain Masters can better their disciple's situation through a single glance, so as to preserve him from ruin

1424- Others are even able to do so though their disciple is quietly sitting somewhere else

1425- However the basic condition of any benefit and favour - and this is unanimously agreed on - lays in the disciple's perfect sincerity and pure intention,

1426- And in his resolved attachment to his Saint Master - *Bliss to thee, o Resolute disciple!*

1427- Any that fastens himself [to such Godly Men] with sincerity and love, will rejoice in the Hereafter

---

supplication to God, and the stone was moved aside for them is recorded in the *Sahih* of Bukhari and Muslim. And the famous hadith recorded by Bukhari and others about the story of Khubayb Al-Ansārī (God be Well Pleased with him) a Companion of the Prophet, of whom Bint Harith said: *"By God, I never saw a better prisoner than Khubayb. By God, one day I found him eating from a bunch of grapes in his hand, though he was manacled in irons and there was no fruit in all of Makkah"*.

1428- Is there something surprising about? No, since such men have reached GOD's Neighbourhood thanks to their sincerity (*Ṣidq*), their exclusive and pure worship (*Ikhlãs*), and their perfect Sense of Ethics (*Adab*)

1429- May GOD rank us amongst those who have faith in everything they assert

1430- And may He incite us to love them all and any who is following them

1431- ...By the Grace of the [Prophet Aḥmad], the Master of Humankind - *Peace and Blessings be upon him for aye*

1432- Let us now resume the enumeration of the causes of ruin we started on[228]

---

[228] This last part poses somehow the much controversial question of the possibility of the Saintly Persons' Intercession in favour of their devotees in the Hereafter inasmuch as it may seem to run counter some rigorous Koranic assertions ("*On that Day no intercession will avail*", "*No soul will bear the burden of another*" and so). However, besides such verses one has also to take into account other verses and Authentic Prophetic Maxims (the opponents of *Taṣawwuf* never makes bones about quoting quite oddly) mitigating a bit the radical impossibility of any kind of intercession for the Believers. Here is a set of verses, of Prophetic maxims and of writings which relate to the question of intercession (here below and in the Hereafter):

"*And those whom they invoke besides GOD have no power of intercession; **only he who bears witness to the truth**, and with full knowledge.*" (Qur-ãn xliii. 86) Yusuf Ali's commentary of this verse is: "*While idols and false gods have no power of intercession, persons like Jesus, who is falsely worshipped by his misguided followers, but who himself preached the Gospel of unity with full understanding, will have the power of intercession*" "*None shall have the power of intercession, **but such a one has received permission** (or promise) from [GOD] Most Gracious* "(Qur-ãn xix. 87) "*No intercession can avail with Him, **except for those for whom He has granted permission**.*" (Qur-ãn xxxiv. 23) "*The Day that the spirit and the angels will stand forth in ranks, none shall speak **except any who is permitted** by The Most Gracious, and he will say what is right.*" (Qur-ãn lxxviii. 37-38) "*What! Do they take for intercessors others besides GOD? Say:* "*Even if they have no power*

196

whatever and no intelligence? " *Say:* "To GOD belongs exclusively **(the right to grant) intercession:** to Him belongs the domination of the heavens and the earth. In the end, it is to Him that ye shall be brought back. "(Qur-ān xxxix. 43-44) *"And they say:* " The Most Gracious has taken a son." *Glory to Him! They are (but) servants raised to honour. They speak not before He speaks, and they acts (in all things) by His Command. He knows what is before them and what is behind them. And they offer no intercession **except for those with whom He is well-pleased** and they stand in awe and reverence of His (Glory)"* (Qur-ān xxi. 26) *"On the day we shall call together all human beings **with their (respective) Imam,** those who are given their record in their right hand will read it (with pleasure), and they will not be dealt with unjustly in the least."* (Qur-ān xvii. 71) *"And when the plague fell on them, they said:* "O Moses! **On our behalf call on thy Lord** in virtue of his promise to thee."(Qur-ān vii.134) *"But some of the Bedouin Arabs believe in GOD and the last day, and look on their payments as pious gifts bringing them nearer to GOD and **obtaining the prayers of the messenger.** Aye, indeed they bring them nearer (to him): soon will GOD admit them to His Mercy: for GOD is Oft-forgiving, Most merciful."* (Qur-ān ix. 99) *" Of their wealth take alms, that so thou mightest purify and sanctify them. And pray on their behalf; verily **thy prayers are source of security for them.**"* (Qur-ān ix.102-103) *"But GOD was not going to send them a chastisement **whilst thou wast amongst them;** nor was He going to send it whilst they could ask for pardon."* (Qur-ān viii. 33) *"And those who came after they say:* "Our Lord! Forgive us, **and our brethren who came before us** into the faith" (Qur-ān lix. 10) *"We send not a Messenger, but to be obeyed, in accordance with the leave of GOD. If they had only, when they were unjust to themselves, come unto thee and asked GOD's forgiveness. And **the Messenger had asked Forgiveness for them,** they would have found GOD indeed Oft-returning, Most Merciful."* (Qur-ān iv. 64) *"And when it is said to them:* "Come, the Messenger of GOD will **pray for your forgiveness**", *they turn aside their heads, and thou wouldst see them turning away their faces in arrogance."* (Qur-ān lxiii. 5) *"They said:* "O father! **Ask for us forgiveness** for our sins, for we were truly at fault." *He said:* "Soon **will I ask my Lord for forgiveness for you:** for He is indeed Oft-forgiving, Most Merciful." (Qur-ān xii. 97-98) *"Their Messenger said to them:* "True, we are human like yourselves, but GOD doth grant **His grace to such of his servants as He pleases.** It is not for us to bring you an authority except as GOD Permits. And on GOD let all men of faith put their trust." (Qur-ān iv. 11)

In *Iḥyā 'Ulūmi-d-Dīn* the Imam Al-Ghazāli reported these following Hadiths: *"On the Judgement Day GOD will call out the Pious and those who fought in His Path so they enter Paradise. The Men of knowledge will then say:* "It was with the help of our knowledge that they succeeded in worshipping and in fighting."

Claiming Fraudulently Saintliness

1433- [One may also count among pernicious misconducts]:

d- Pretending fraudulently to be a Saintly Person or claiming to work miracles in order to be revered by people

---

GOD will tell them: "I raise you to the Dignity of the Angels; do intercede in their favour so they may obtain Mine." *Thus will they enter Heaven."* The Prophet (PBH) said: "*Three kinds of persons will be granted permission to intercede on the Last Day: the Prophets, the [Righteous] Scholars and the Martyrs*". We may still read in Al-Ghazāli's book: "*The Believer must give credit to the final leaving of Hell of all the monotheists; for no one who believe in GOD's Unity will abide eternally in the Fire. He must also have faith in the intercession of the Prophets, that of the Scholars, the Martyrs and the other Believers according to their respective Degrees before GOD. The rest of the Believers who will not get an intercessor will eventually get out of Hell by the Divine Grace.*" In a hadith reported by Muslim, the Messenger (PBH) said: "*Whoever invoke GOD to impart me the Degree of Wasila (means of access to GOD) will benefit from my intercession on the Resurrection Day.*" He also said: "*I swear by Whom in Whose Hands is my soul that there will be a time when Hell's Gates will be shut and when watercress will grow on its ground*". *GOD will then say: "The Angels, the Prophets and the Believers have all interceded for the sinners and now there is none to intercede for these except the MOST MERCIFUL of those who show mercy." So will HE take a handful of fire and will get out of Hell a people who never performed a single good deed."*

We may also read in <u>The Reliance of the Traveller</u> of the Sheikh Aḥmad ibn Naqib al-Misri: " *It is obligatory to believe in the intercession of the Prophet, then that of the religious Scholars, of the Martyrs and of other believers; the intercession of each one commensurates with his rank and position with GOD MOST HIGH. Any believer remaining in hell without intercessor shall be taken out of it by the favour of GOD, and anyone with an atom's weight of faith in his heart will eventually depart from it.*"

After the reading of such verses, a-*hadith* and writings one must assuredly admit that it is more likely to uphold a happy medium and adopt a more balanced position, that is (1) rejecting the laxity of those who persevere in wrong-doing while confiding thoughtlessly in some assistance Tomorrow, (2) acknowledging that the Divine Mercy will permit some among the Chosen Congregation to intercede on the behalf of the Believers who will deserve it. But GOD knows better…

1434- To any who sincerely wants to attain perfection, I advise him [to act clear-sightedly] and to keep company with the perfect and *authentic* Saints

1435- Because it is quite obvious that nowadays the most of the so-called "sheikhs" are just deceitful rogues

1436- Some of them, that are inordinately greedy for honours, rush towards worldly power without any scruple[229]

1437- ...And without even their being in the least able to discriminate *Farāid* (Obligatory acts of Worship) from *Sunān* (Traditional acts); indeed these are misleading people straight towards sources of ordeals

1438- Such villains, who pride themselves on perfection and saintliness, never cease showering people with endless and idle quotations!

1439- Whenever thou happen to praise another Sheikh before one of them, he chokes of anger, out of envy and of liking for pre-eminence!

1440- Conversely, if ever thou disparage another Master he becomes delighted, even if that concerns a Master whose virtues are well-renowned

1441- Naught would ever gladden his heart but remaining the only one to be mentioned and praised by his fellow creatures

---

[229]Cf. Qur-ān ix. 34-35: "*O ye who believe! There are indeed many among the priests and anchorites, who in falsehood devour the wealth of men and hinder (them) from the way of GOD. And there are those who hoard gold and silver and spend it not in the way of GOD: announce unto them a most grievous chastisement. On the Day when it will be heated in the fire of Hell, and with it will be branded their foreheads, their flanks, and their backs,* "This is the (treasure) which ye hoarded for yourselves: taste ye then, the (treasures) ye hoarded""

1442- In case thou choose another Master to guide thee unto the Right Path, he feels irritated [and starts to belittle him]

1443- Woe to him! If he was sincerely and solely interested in that disciple's Salvation

1444- ...He would certainly have been delighted by the prospect of his success, wherever he may find it, and he would not have been so bothered by his departure

1445- Know that the "sheikhs" of this kind are just pursuing earthly purposes [as wealth and authority]- *flee thou far from them!*

1446- Any amongst the would-be "sheikhs" thou see behaving as he was superior to all the servants of GOD [is a swindler] - do keep away from him, o thou *Murīd* [that is searching for a *bona fide* Master]

1447- [And call to thy mind that] GOD's Grace is not restricted or reserved [to just few creatures out of the rest]; He does impart His Gifts to whomsoever He pleases amongst the human beings[230]

1448- Indeed there is a valuable teaching in this popular maxim:*"Never will an envious man be superior to anyone""*

1449- How could he be *superior* [and achieve his aim] since such an aim is all his believing brethren be deprived of their favours!

1450- Thou may often see some [of those *tartuffes*] turbaned with their faces meticulously veiled

1451- ...Trying thereby to look like the Virtuous Spiritual Leaders whose sole and constant concern were gaining GOD's Satisfaction

---

[230]*Cf.* Qur-ān xvii. 20: "*Of the bounties of thy LORD we bestow freely on all-these as well as those: the bounties of thy LORD are not closed (to anyone).*"

1452- [Such sanctimonious hypocrites] mention very often the Holy Name of GOD with their *tongues* whereas their very *hearts* remain among the most corrupt in the world

1453- They display showily rigorous asceticism through which they are just aiming at material goods [and at glamour] - *waken thou [o Murīd!]*

1454- Some of those sham "masters" claim to eat not land produce and hide perfidiously their game

1455- Thus do they try to be likened to [the Virtuous *Sufis*] who are striving against their lust and whose sole objective is their LORD

1456- Nonetheless, if such rascals happen to be hungry and to remain alone before a bowl of bran, they would not hesitate to stuff up themselves therewith! - *mind to beware of them*

1457- They ignore certainly that eating licit land produce - just as "the common run of people" are doing - is regarded as praiseworthy in Islamic Law (*Shari'a*)[231]

1458- Thou may also see some of those Pharisees refusing to look at women and keeping their eyes modestly lowered

1459- ...Trying in so doing to impersonate the Eminent Masters - those who put rigorously their knowledge into practice, those who are self-restrained and upright because of their fear of GOD

1460- However - were it not people's eyes - such libertines would not hesitate in the least to set dealings with those women-folk for fornication and other indecencies!

---

[231] *Cf.* Qur-ān v. 88: "*Eat to the things which GOD hath provided for you, lawful and good; but fear GOD in Whom ye believe.*"

1461- Some others claim to have attained GOD's Neighbourhood (<u>H</u>a<u>d</u>ratu-l-Lāh): the reason for which they gave up any act of worship - so do they perish!

1462- They have been deluded by their lack of understanding and by the veil of their sins which hide the Truth from them

1463- Because they have misinterpreted the word "yaqīn" in the last verse of the Sūrah Al-Hijr [in construing it etymologically; that is to say: "certainty"] whereas its true meaning here is "death"[232]

1464- [O thou that is seeking for GOD!] as long as thou find not a True and Virtuous Master, do content thyself with the teaching handed on us by the Noble Ancients in their priceless works

1465- Such a Legacy is: [the perfect compliance] with the Law of the Messenger, the Chosen *Par Excellence - may he be granted Peace and Blessings by the OFT-FORGIVING LORD*

1466- Then neither act *under* the limits of the Law [in fulfilling not the legal conditions of worship] (*ifrā<u>t</u>*) nor act *beyond* them [in exceeding thoughtlessly the legal restrictions out of zeal] (*tafrī<u>t</u>*), but always remain justly balanced according to the *Sunna* of the Prophet[233]

1467- It has been said that keeping perfectly upright within the strict limits of the Law is the Height of Virtue and Worthiness

---

[232]The verse in question is: "*And serve thy LORD until there come unto thee* Yaqīn *(the Hour that is Certain; death)*" (xv. 99) The construction disparaged here by the Sheikh would imply that man is compelled to worship the LORD until he reaches the state of True "Certainty", stage after which he would no longer be subject to adoration!

[233]*Cf.* Qur-ān ii. 143 "*Thus have We made of you an* Ummat *[Community] justly balanced, that ye might be witnesses over the nations (...)*" Islam is, *par excellence*, the Religion of balance and justice, this unlike the common inaccurate idea too hastily conveyed by ill-informed or ill-intentioned persons. And no one can fully appreciate this but who has been granted clear-sightedness by the MOST GRACIOUS LORD Who makes him see or experience how illusory and fleeting are human conceptions if not inspired by Divine Breath...

1468- Trust not any who appears under the features of a "sheikh" in our times

1469- [Beware!] All that is round [and coloured] is not necessarily a cake and all spot of light is not the moon

1470- Nay! Any water is not of *Salsabīl*[234] Indeed acid and honey are not at all alike - o shrewd Man! *[wilt thou not beware?]*

1471- All that is glowing in the darkness of the night is not necessarily a fire which a wayfarer can warm himself with

1472- Do always examine closely a man before keeping company with him and never choose an insane or a self-interested person as a companion

1473- Thou canst happen sometimes to despise a servant who is yet endowed with priceless spiritual advantages

1474- Then never look down on a servant of GOD owing to his humble clothes or his lowly and slovenly appearance

1475- How many who appear insignificant although their being filled with the Lights [of knowledge] and with Wondrous Divine Secrets!

1476- And how many who appear worthy and meritorious before people's eyes and who are regarded, wherever they pass, as the "Poles of the Universe"

1477- ...And whose renown travels throughout the world whereas their actual spiritual degree equals that of a *monkey* before the MOST GRACIOUS!

---

[234]A fountain in Paradise (*Cf.* Qur-ān lxxvi. 18)

1478- Let us complete here the part devoted to the rules of *adab* and tackle now [the last part of this book] dealing with the marvellous Surã of the Qur-ãn [and other useful pleas and invocations]

Invocations to God
(Ãdãb) [235]

1319/20- [The prior conditions] of effectual invocations are:

❶ Avoiding illicit food and drink,

❷ Avoiding improper speech,

❸ Avoiding wearing indecent or soiled clothes,

❹ Worshipping sincerely and exclusively [GOD], *to Whom belong flesh and soul as well*

1321/22- It is also recommended

❶ To precede one's invocations by pious deeds [like giving alms],

❷ To perform ablutions,

❸ To clean the invocation place,

❹ To accomplish two rak'a,

❺ To kneel down with one's face turned towards the Ka'ba - *all of these are verily valued*

1323/25- [When beginning actually invocations] the servant has

❶ To praise the MERCIFUL LORD[236],

---

[235]Mind not to confuse the transcription *ãdãb* (invocations) with that of *adab* (Ethics)

[236]In saying *"Alḥamdu li-Lãhi Rabbi-l-'Ãlamĩn"* (Praise be to GOD, the CHERISHER and SUSTAINER of the Worlds!)

❷ To call for Blessings upon the Holy Prophet - [Note that this _Salāt 'alā Nabī_] must be said as well at the beginning as at the end of the invocations -

❸ To raise his hands wide-open heavenwards and level with his shoulders,

❹ To keep correct and in awe for GOD, like an imploring beggar,

❺ To call in his mind GOD's Wondrous Attributes,

❻ To feel infinitely humble and weak [in comparison with Him][237]

1326- Who that intends to make invocations has to use the Fine and Glorious Names of GOD (_Asmāu-l-Husnā_) and the pleas reported from [the Messenger], the Best of humankind

1327- ...Or other entreaties taken from the Virtuous Ancients, as the Companions of the Prophet and the Eminent Sheikhs

1328- He must also implore the LORD - _Who that begins the process of creation_ (Al-Badīu) _and that repeats it_ (Al-Mu'īdu) - and pray through the intermediary of His Prophets and that of the Virtuous Servants (_tawasul_)[238]

---

[237]_Cf._ Qur-ān vii. 55-56: "_Call on your LORD with humility and in private: for GOD loveth not those who trespass beyond bounds. Do not mischief on the earth, after it hath been set in order, but call on Him with fear and longing (in your hearts): for the Mercy of GOD is (always) near to those who do good._"

[238]The question concerning the lawfulness of _Tawasul_ (calling upon the righteous or praying through their intermediary), of its being not a kind of _Shirk_ (assigning partners to GOD) has always divided, in Islam, the partisans of pure _Shari'a_ and that of pure _haqīqah_ (schematically talking). We may find an extract confirming its quite legitimacy in The Reliance of the Traveller (_Muddatu-s-Sālik_) of the Sheikh Ahmad ibn Naqib al-Misri (p.939-940): "... _As for calling upon the righteous_ [note: when they are physically absent, as in the

1329- In a low and humble voice; he must admit plainly all his sins and [whenever he asks for some favour] he will have to pray first for himself [before extending the prayers to the whole Community][239]- *so as to not be deprived of benefits*

1330- However concerning an Imam, he is not allowed to give greater importance to his own person in his supplications; he has the obligation to make pleas for all the Community

---

words "O Mu_h_ammad" in the above hadīths-], tawasul *to GOD MOST HIGH through them is permissible; the supplication (du'a) being to GOD MOST GLORIOUS, and there is much evidence for its permissibility. Those who call on them intending* tawasul *cannot be blamed. As for some who believes that that those called upon can cause effects, benefit, or harm, which they create or cause to exist as GOD does, such a person is an idolater who has left Islam- GOD be our refuge! A certain person has written an article that* tawasul *to GOD MOST HIGH through the righteous is unlawful, while the overwhelming majority of scholars hold it as permissible, and the evidence the writer uses to corroborate his point of view is devoid of anything that demonstrate what he is trying to prove. In declaring* tawasul *permissible we are not hovering on the brink of idolatry* (shirk) *or coming anywhere near it, for the conviction that GOD MOST HIGH alone has influence over anything, outwardly or inwardly, is a conviction that flows through us like our very lifeblood. If* tawasul *were idolatry* (shirk) *or if there were any suspicion of idolatry in it, the Prophet (GOD MOST HIGH bless him and give him peace) would not have taught it the blind man when the latter asked him to supplicate GOD for him, though in fact he did teach him to make* tawasul *to GOD through him. And the notion that* tawasul *is permissible only during the lifetime of the person through whom it is done but not after his death is not supported by any viable foundation from Sacred Law..."*

[239]Though Islam preaches concern for the entire Community it admits however that man's inherent tendency leads him to prefer his own person above all. This even if Islam differs radically as well from individualistic attitude advocated in Western culture as from the doctrinal extremism of Socialism, in reconciling general and individual interest through the quest of personal salvation -"*The Day when no soul shall have power to do aught for another*"(lxxxii. 19) - through social concern -Community Obligations and the like.

1331- Express thy wishes over and over, be thou steadfast and persevering[240], remain concentrated and hopeful [about the outcome of thy request]

1332- Do strive thereon, o thou that art shrewd!, and never make prayers for unlawful purposes,

1333- ...Or for something that is already and fully accomplished or which is outside the realms of possibility; make no restriction [in excluding deliberately a Muslim Brother from thy prayer] and never pray for aught that will entail conflicts[241]

1334- Show not haste or impatience and never say: ***Surely my prayer will not be answered***" - never lose hope [in GOD's Mercy]

1335/36- [The rules of invocations also imply]
    ❼ Expressing any serious need

    ❽ Saying "āmīn" (amen) [at the end] by who that is imploring and all who hear him

    ❾ Passing one's two palms on the face by way of a final touch

1337- Whoever complies perfectly with all these rules, while offering his prayers to GOD, will obtain Satisfaction without any possible doubt

---

[240]*Cf.* Qur-ān ii. 45: "*Seek (GOD 's) Help with patient perseverance and prayer: it is indeed hard, except to those who are humble.*"
[241]Lit. " anything that will entail the breaking of kinship bonds"...

Times when Prayers are mostly Granted

1338/39- Times when GOD is more likely to answer pleas are - according to the True Knowers (*'ārifīn*):

❶ The entire month of Fast (*Ramaḍān*)[242],

❷ The Day of 'Arafāt[243],

❸ The Night of Power and Honour (*Laylatu-l-Qadr*)[244],

❹ Every Thursday night,

❺ Every Friday,

❻ Friday *blessed time*

1340- There is some divergence among the Erudite and Honourable Masters as to know when is exactly located such a *blessed time*

1341- Some assert that it takes place as soon as the Imam sits [in the *Miḥrāb* prior to leading Friday Prayer] and ends when the prayer is completed

---

[242]The 9th month of Islamic calendar which is also the month when the Qur-ān was first revealed, - highly sacred in Islam.

[243]The 9th of *Dhul-hijja* (the month of Pilgrimage and the last of Islamic calendar).

[244]Cf. Sūrah xcvii: "*We have indeed revealed this (Qur-ān) in the Night of Power...*" The exact location of this day arouses some divergences between the Scholars even if it is commonly agreed that it takes place in the last days of the month of *Ramaḍān*. The Prophet never gave a definite day but contented himself in giving few particulars about. Let us content ourselves with a calendar established by the Ancients we found in some book of the Sheikh. According to it the fixing of the night of *Laylatu-l-Qadr* is not definitive and has to be determined depending on the very day when the fast starts. So if the fast begins a Monday, *Laylatu-l-Qadr* has to be celebrated the 19th of *Ramaḍān* and so forth (see Tome IV, Annex 3 at www.majalis.org/masalik)

1342- Others say that Friday *blessed time* lapses during the reciting of the two *Fātiḥa*[245] by the Imam - *[but GOD wot better]*

1343/50- [Other times of *Ijābah* (pleas granting) are]
   ❼ Dead of night,

   ❽ The second half of night[246],

   ❾ Dawn (*saḥar*),

   ❿ The last two thirds of the night,

   ⓫ During performance of Canonical Prayers,

   ⓬ While the public Call to prayer (*Nidā*)[247] is performed,

   ⓭ The interval of time within the Call and the Prayer Announcement (*Iqāmah*)[248],

   ⓮ When the phrase "*Ḥayy 'alā Ṣalāh*[249]" is uttered [twice during the public Call] - such a moment is particularly favourable [for making a wish] for any strained, despairing or forceless person,

---

[245]"The Opening Chapter", Qur-ān i.

[246]Which has to be calculated knowing sunset time and dawn time, which correspond respectively to the Sunset Prayer (*Maghrib*) and the Morning Prayer (*Subḥ*).

[247] This is a Traditional Practice performed in every mosque or muslim assembly consisting in these words: "*GOD is the GREATEST!* (twice) *I testify that there is no deity but GOD!* (twice) *I testify that Muḥammad is GOD's Messenger!* (twice) *Hasten ye to the prayer!* (twice) *Hasten ye to the Bliss!* (twice) *GOD is the GREATEST!* (twice) *There is no deity but GOD!*"

[248] The *Iqāmah* is the short speech pronounced by the *Nāim* (the Imam's auxiliary) when Believers are lining up for the prayer. Its content is nearly the same as that of the *Nidā*.

[249]"*Hasten ye to the prayer!*"

❶❺ When Muslims are forming rows during Holy War or before Canonical prayer,

❶❻ Just after Canonical Prayers,

❶❼ During the mêlée [when the battle against unbelievers is at its height],

❶❽ Right after the reading of the Qur-ãn, mostly during the recitation of the _Khitm_[250],

❶❾ When one is drinking Zam-Zam water[251],

❷⓿ After the Imam has pronounced the last words of the _Fātiḥa_:"_wa la ḍālīn._" during a Muslim assembly on a [lawful] purpose,

❷⓿ While closing the eyes of a just-dead person,

❷❷ When rain is falling,

❷❸ When the cock is crowing,

❷❹ During _Dhikr_ performance.

---

[250]Lit. "the seal"; an extra text appearing traditionally at the end of the Book and which consists in pleas.
[251]See notes corresponding to verse 1351.

Places where Prayers are more likely to be Granted

1351/55- Regarding such Blessed Places, we count:

❶ All around the Ka'ba, when the *tawāf*[252] is performed [during Pilgrimage],

❷ At Multazam[253],

❸ The place [in Makkah] from where one can see for the first time our LORD's Sacred House [the Ka'ba],

❹ [Whenever thou read the Qur-ãn] and reach the "Two Majesties" (*Jalãlatayn*)[254],

❺ Inside the Ka'ba,

❻ In front of the well of Zam-zam,

❼ At the two Hills of Safã and Marwa[255],

❽ During the walk between those two places,

---

[252]The going round the Ka'ba seven times any Pilgrim has to perform and during which he kisses the Black Stone.

[253] That is the place between the gates of Makkah and the Black Stone.

[254]Qur-ãn vi. 124 where we may exceptionally find twice the word "*GOD*", placed side by side without any other word between. When we come to the 1st *GOD*, we have to stop and make a wish before passing to the next "*GOD*" and going on reading...

[255] Two little hills in the city of Makkah where the pilgrim has to go. Their story is closely connected with that of the well of Zam-Zam where, according to tradition, the lady Hãjar, mother of the infant Ismãĩl, prayed for water in the parched desert. In her eager quest round these two hills, she found her prayer answered and saw the Zam-zam spring...Cf. Qur-ãn ii. 158: " *Behold! Safa and Marwa are among the Symbols of GOD.*"

❾ Just after the *Maqām Ibrāhīm*[256],

❿ In Mina,

⓫ In 'Arafāt,

⓬ During the three symbolic stonings (*Jamrah*),

⓭ At the graves of the Prophets, of the Saints and of the Virtuous creatures[257]

---

[256]The Station of Abraham. *Cf.* Qur-ān ii.125: " *Remember We made the House [the Ka'ba] a place of assembly for men and a place of safety; and take ye the Station of Abraham as a place of prayer.*"

[257] As for visiting the graves of Godly Persons and invoking GOD thereat, there is some divergence about its permissibility among the different currents of Islam. Let us quote in this instance some interesting passages of The Reliance of the Traveller: "*[It is offensive] to place an inscription on a tomb [whether it is the name of the deceased or something other on a board at the head of the grave or on something else; unless the deceased is a Friend of God* (wali) *or a religious scholar, in which case his name is written so that he may be visited and honored].*" "*[As for the Tomb of the Prophet Mu*ẖ*ammad]: It is commended to pray two rak'as to greet his mosque, and then approach the noble and honoured tomb and stand at the head of it with one's back to the direction of prayer* (qibla). *One bows one's head and summons to mind reverent awe and humility, then greets the Prophet* (PBH) *and blesses him in a normal voice:* "Peace be upon you, o Messenger of God..." *After which one supplicates God for whatever one wishes. Then one step half a meter to the right to greet Abu Bakr, and again to the right to greet 'Umar* (APT). *Then it is recommended to return to one's original place and do much of supplicating God, turning to God through the Prophet* (PBH) (tawasul) *(concerning one's aims and goals, since he is the greatest intermediary in intercession and other things), and invoking blessings upon him....It is unlawful to circumbulate the tomb. It is offensive to nudge the wall around the tomb with one's back or front, to kiss it or touch it (with one's hand). Proper conduct here is to stand back from it as one would if present during his life* (PBH). *This is what is right and what scholars have said and are agreed upon. One should not be deceived by what some common people do in their ignorance of proper manners for it is reprehensible innovation* (bid'a). "

The question of praying near Saintly Men's graves is more generally connected with that of obtaining blessings (*tabarruk*) through the Righteous

Persons whose Prayers are Granted

1356/61- As for persons whose pleas GOD is more likely to answer, one may count:

❶ A [faithful] poor,

❷ Any sincere Muslim,

❸ Any person victim of a glaring injustice [and who calls on GOD's Arbitration], be he an unbeliever

---

which is also a very controversial issue. So may we read thereon in The Reliance of the Traveller (p. 320): " *To hold that things have properties that can benefit or harm independently of the Will of God is unbelief* (kufr), *whether such properties are considered natural or supernatural. But the contention of certain people that showing veneration* (ta'zim) *for the righteous or that obtaining blessings* (tabarruk) *through them or their effects constitutes worship of them or associating others with God* (shirk) *is not supportable by the Prophetic Sunna, which attests to the contrary, as may be seen from the following hadiths:*

⁽1⁾*Bukhari relates that Uthman ibn Abdullah said:* "My wife sent me to Umm Salama with a cup of water in which to dip a look containing some of the Prophet's hair (PBH). Whenever a person was suffering from the evil eye or an illness, they would send her a vessel of water [which Umm Salama would dip the hair in, for treating the ill by their drinking it or washing with it]. I looked into the metal bell [holding the look of hair] and saw some red hairs."

⁽2⁾*Bukhari relates from Abu Musa that* "The Prophet (PBH) called for a vessel of water, washed his hands and face in it spat a mouthful of water back into it and then said to Abu Musa and Bilal *'Drink from it and pour the rest over your faces and chests* "

⁽3⁾*Bukhari relates from Muhammad Ibn Rabi that* "When the Prophet (PBH) performed his ablutions, the Companions almost fought over the excess water".

The Prophet (PBH) would never have permitted the like of this if there were any suspicion of associating partners with God (shirk) in it. In each of the above hadith and others there is a clear basis for the legal validity of obtaining blessings through the effects of the Righteous (tabarruk), *as it was done with the Prophet's consent and with the Companions, this being the reason why Muslims after them have also done so. And God knows best."*

❹ A caring father that is praying for his children[258],

❺ Any steadfast and virtuous person[259],

❻ A wayfarer,

❼ Who that is fasting,

❽ A fair and kind Imam,

❾ A devoted son praying for his Muslim parents,

❿ Who that has genuinely repented of his sins,

⓫ A Muslim who is praying for the good of his fellow Believers out of any ostentation...

1362- By this comes to an end what concerns invocations.
Let us now resume [in verses] the chapter devoted to our Master Al-Deymānī's prose work

---

[258]If nevertheless these are Muslims otherwise it is not permitted in Islam to pray for one's unbelieving kin. *Cf.* the story of Abraham's father, that of the son and the wife of Noah and so. Qur-ān ix. 113 "*It is not fitting for the Prophet and those who believe, that they should pray for forgiveness for Pagans, even though they be of kin, after it is clear to them that they are companions of the Fire. And Abraham prayed for his father's forgiveness only because of a promise he had made to him. But when it became clear to him that he was an enemy to GOD, he dissociated himself from him: for Abraham was most tender heart, forbearing...*" See also xi:45-47; xlvi:10

[259]*Cf.* Qur-ān xlii. 26-27: "*And He listens to those who believe and do deeds of righteousness, and gives them increase of His Bounty.*"

Wird Practice

267- If ever thou art unaware of the principle of *wird* practice[260], do know that its purpose is most valuable

268- [An evidence thereon is] its ranking amongst the most eminent of well-established pious deeds by all [that know]

269- Its definition is "an act of worship regularly performed at a given time of the day"

270- Its etymology is connected with the desert travellers' habit to make regular stops at watering points for supply

271- Each of the existing *wird* can lead, with no deviation, towards GOD's Neighbourhood (*Hadratu-l-Lāh*) any servant that performs it daily [in accordance with the special rules related to their practice]

272- And it matters little that such a *wird* originated from Sheikh Abd-al-Qadīr Jīlānī[261] or from Sheikh Ahmad Tijānī[262]

273- ...Or from any amongst the other eminent *Qutb*[263]; because all of them are in the Right Path

---

[260] *Wird* practice arose about the twelfth century (AD.) when the *turūq* (plur. of *tarīqa*: Islamic brotherhoods) took the habit of imposing to their disciples the repetition of some particular orisons. Thus, the *wird* is a liturgy which helps in preparing the heart for the Remembrance of GOD's Holy Names (*Dhikr*) through series of traditional pleas, of Koranic verses and of various invocations one has to repeat a several times everyday.

[261] Founder of the *Qadriyya*, the most ancient and biggest Islamic *tarīqa* (see Tome IV, Annex 1 at www.majalis.org/masalik).

[262] Founder of the *Tijāniyya*, another great Islamic brotherhood (see Tome IV, Annex 1 at www.majalis.org/masalik).

[263]*Cf.* note 6.

274- And all of them prompt their disciples unto worshipping the LORD OF THE THRONE

275- …And unto what is upright; thence beware of ever belittling any of the accredited *wird* and never denigrate one of them[264]

276- The true origin of a *wird* is either the Revelation or the Inspiration reserved by [GOD], the SOURCE OF PEACE, for the servants HE has chosen

277- In case of Revelation (*wahy*) that concerns a Prophet but if conveyed through Inspiration (*Ilham*) that is intended for a Saint[265]

278- As for the *wird* content, it consists in gathered extracts taken from GOD's Revealed Book [the Qur-ãn] and in Prophetic pleas transmitted through a chain of accredited reporters

279- Know thou that every Saint holds on mystically to the tail of a Prophet sent by [GOD], the TRUTH, the ONLY ONE

---

[264] Commenting verses 271 to 275, F. Dumond wrote, in his book La Pensée Religieuse d'Amadou Bamba (p.98):"*These verses are u defintive refutation against all who supposed or thought up conflicts and compromises between Amadou Bamba and the other brotherhoods' leaders concerning the question of* Wird. We saw the accusations brought against the Sheikh Al-Khadîm *in this regard. Whereas [we may see through these verses that] the Sheikh does not only respect impartially the* wird *of the* Qadriyya *and that of the* Tijaniyya *but he extends such a respect to all the other* wirds, *provided they emanate from an authentic* Qutb, *that is to say a well-established spiritual Master.*"

[265] *Cf.* this hadith we may read in The Reliance of the Traveller (*Muddatu-s-Sãlik*) of the Sheikh Ahmad ibn Naqib al-Misri (p. 1015): "*Muslim relates in his Sahih from A'isha that the Prophet (PBH) said:* "There used to be in the nations before you those who were spoken to. If there are any in my community, 'Umar Ibn Khattab is one of them ". *But this intuition* (ilham) *does not equal the divine inspiration* (wahy) *in strength (of certainly) because of the possibility that what is apprehended by the Friend of God* (wali) *is merely thoughts of his own mind.*"

280- Thenceforth any miracle (*Mu'jizat*) accomplished by a Prophet may well be repeated in the form of a marvel (*Karāmat*) by a Saint

281- For this last [the Saint] represents the true heir of that first [the Prophet]. As regarding the Prophets, they stand for our LORD's arguments against HIS creatures[266] - *know thou that*

282- Whilst the Saints are the evidence that HIS Words are Truthful and that HIS Religion is authentic

283- The Prophets of the MOST HIGH are held impeccable whereas HIS Saints are granted Protection and Worthiness

284- Thence all the Prophets and the Saints are under the Safeguard of the MOST GRACIOUS - *as we hold it from those who are versed in Gnosis*

285- Nonetheless the kind of Safeguard ensured to the Prophets is necessary [given their mission and status] unlike that of the Saints

286- These clarifications are given by the Sheikh Sayd al-Mukhtār Kuntiyu, in his work called "*Al-Kawkab-al-Waqqād*" (The Luminous Planet) - *mistrust not his words*

287- If thou happenst to go for a *wird*, perform it with consideration and due regard for its special conditions - *so wilt thou gain greatest advantages*

288- As for he that denigrates any importance or usefulness of *wird* practice, mocking thereto out of reluctance or scorn

289- ...Such a one is, of a certain, a narrow-minded ignoramus - as conveyed by the witty remarks of the Distinguished Ibn 'Atā, in his work entitled "*Al-Hikam*" (Pieces of Wisdom)

---

[266]*Cf.* Qur-ān xvi. 89: " *On the day We shall raise from all peoples a witness against them, from amongst themselves: and We shall bring thee [O Prophet!] as a witness against these (thy people)(...)* "

290- Any such who resolves not to perform a *wird* and, so, goes on dissipating his lifetime [in some less profitable activities]

291- ...Shall win naught, on the Day of Rewarding, but sorrow, pain and sadness

292- Because no one would disdain the advantages deriving from *wird* practice but such a one that is filled with jealousy, with hatred and resentment [for true worshippers]

293- [What!] How can we scorn the Repetition of GOD's Fine Names, regularly and continuously performed by one of His Servants!

294- All who have not been trained by a competent Master will assuredly come up against terrible ordeals

295- Because any that is deprived of an enlightened Guide, Satan shall unavoidably lead him [headlong unto the Depths of Perdition], whatever his wish may be

296- If thou art prevented from going for a *wird* out of laziness, do not run down its merit [or look down those who practise it] out of resentment

297- " If thou feel unable to cover the gap towards the *watering point*, try not to dissuade others from going and quenching their thirst, my Brother"

298- Know moreover that the level of thy Rewarding depends on the number of *wirds* thou performed in reverence and meditation

Dhikr Practice

299- As for *Dhikr* regular performance, that is indeed the best deed to which a GOD-seeker (*Al- Murīd*)[268] may devote himself

---

[267] *Dhikr* constitutes the main religious practice in *Tasawwuf*. The Arabic word "*Dhikr*" encompasses as well an idea of "recollection", "remembrance" as the meaning of "making mention", "utterance"... Such a practice can be defined, according to the Mystics, as the assiduous repetition of GOD's Names, the continuous recollection of GOD and the forgetting of anything but HIM. Its object is to focus entirely the heart towards WHO is mentioned until His Name takes complete possession of it. *Dhikr* regular practice strengthens the soul, penetrates the heart - in accordance with the famous locution "*Dhikr* begins with the tongue and ends with the heart". The main advantage of such a state, which represents its basic principle for *Sūfis*, is to renounce definitely this material world so as to lead an ascetic life and to get nearer the LORD.

[268] *Al-Murīd*: In Sufism this word refers to a novice, a disciple who aspires to get nearer to GOD under the Guidance of an Accredited Spiritual Master (*Shaykh*). That is, in the consecrated hierarchy of the *turūq* (brotherhoods), the "beginner" called *mubtadī*. There is also an idea of volition, of longing in the semantic content of the word *murīd*; the Arabic verbal form *arāda* which originates it means "to want, to long for something", the reason why we translate it by "GOD-seeker".

Nevertheless in Senegal this term is traditionally consecrated to the disciples of Sheikh Ahmadu Bamba whose order - called *Murīdiyya* (Muridism) -has never ceased undergoing the most fierce and spiteful denigration as the French author F. Dumond made notice in his book La Pensée Religieuse d'Amadou Bamba: "*From its very beginning certain persons - more ignorant than ill-intentioned, but having however both of these defects - tried to label the* Muridiyya *as a "sect", that is to say "a group of persons who broke away from a religious community in following a doctrinaire and narrow-minded ideology." Yet there is no point of proving [such iniquitous allegations] because we will demonstrate, through the analysis of* Ahmadu Bamba's *writings, that it is an orthodox Muslim brotherhood, founded by an orthodox Sheikh although his being Mystic"*

300- And I do openly say this without any mysterious periphrasis or the least concern for deniers

301- To any such that would ask me about, I give this plain answer:" [Read thou this verse]:" *The remembrance of GOD* (Dhikr) *is the greatest thing without doubt.*"[269]

302- I do assert that whosoever gives up the Remembrance and the Utterance of GOD's Holy Attributes, in return for the remembrance of aught else, such a one is a whimsical fool, for certain!

303- What! How can the creatures forget or show heedlessness for the Recollection of Whom has created them and has given them shape!

304- Remembering GOD's Attributes represents the first step toward Saintliness and its giving up is the height of going astray[270]

305- May GOD rank us among His Servants who spend their whole lifetime in meditating on His Signs and in repeating His Fine Names[271]

306- However there are differing opinions amongst the Honourable Masters as to know whether it is preferable to utter GOD's Names in a low or loud voice

---

[269]Qur-ān xxix. 45: *"Recite what is sent of the Book by inspiration to thee, and establish regular prayer: for prayer restrains from shameful and evil deeds; and remembrance of GOD is the greatest (thing in life) without doubt. And GOD knows the (deeds) that ye do.* "This verse is, *par excellence,* that which shows *Dhikr* importance; the reason why it is often quoted by *Sūfis.*

[270]Cf. Qur-ān lvii. 16: *"Has not the time arrived for the Believers that their hearts in all humility should engage in the remembrance of GOD and of the Truth which has been revealed (to them)?"*

[271]Cf. Qur-ān vii. 80: *"The Most Beautiful Names* ('Asmāu-l-Husnā) *belong to GOD: so call Him by them."* Qur-ān xx. 8: *"GOD! There is no god but He! To him belong the Most Beautiful Names."*

307- Some give preference to the lowering of the voice in their concern to not lapse into ostentation and to concentrate better for any that is intending to accomplish *Dhikr*

308- Whilst other Masters prefer the raising of the voice so as to transmit its echo to one's neighbouring fellows who might be tempted to imitate so [the *Dhikr* performer]

309- Because whenever someone else happens to do the same, twofold Reward wilt thou be imparted owing to [thy prompting other people unto good deeds]

310- Moreover, given that all human senses have to take part in the Remembrance of the LORD and CHERISHER of Mankind [thy tongue must partake therein as well]

311- Other Scholars have adopted the happy medium of such a divergence in giving these following particulars:

312- If man fears to lapse into ostentation, it behoves to him to lower his voice and to conceal his performance in so doing

313- Because, in this case, his act of worship will be safeguarded against annulment only if fulfilled in discretion and secrecy

314- But if man is free from such a danger, owing to his firmness and his inner purity [conferred by long habit]

315- ...His duty is then to raise his voice so as to gain benefits deriving from imitation

316- This [justly balanced] opinion is that of our Sheikh Al-Mukhtār Kuntiyu - *may GOD, the MAKER, be Well-Pleased with him*

317- Refer - o my Fellow! - to the book "The Shield of the GOD-seeker " by that Upright Leader [for other questions relating to *Dhikr*]

318/321- Are likewise counted amongst the rules of *Dhikr*:

     ≈ Its performance in a clean place

     ≈ Sitting cross-legged or squatting down, as during the prayer

     ≈ Having one's face turned towards the Ka'ba

     ≈ Wearing scent seeing that places where *Dhikr* is performed are necessarily frequented by Angels and Muslim Jinns, who come and listen - as agrees on the Consensus [of the Masters] (*Ijma'*)

322- Belong also to [*Dhikr* requirements] the entire dedication of the deeds to GOD[272]; so the servant has to prevent aught that is not proper to mix therewith

---

[272]*Cf.* Qur-ān xxxix. 11: "*Say:*" Verily, I am commanded to serve GOD with sincere devotion.""

Some Recommendations of the Prophet

as a prologue

1532-1536
"O my Brother! Never be lazy, for life flies swiftly. Do avoid waste of times and eschew thou from such vices as:

Scandalmongering

Ostentation

Self-conceit

Envy

Arrogance

Behaving mercilessly with thy fellow creatures

Liking for people's esteem and for superiority over thy generation.

Any that is combining all of these vices, or that is even endowed with just one of them, will undoubtedly perish. For each of them entails GOD's rejecting every good deed back to his doer - thence have we to be mindful."

1537- This *hadīth* [can be found in a work] of our Master Al-Ghazālī - *may GOD be Satisfied with him for aye -*

1538- ...And has been reported from the Best of the Prophets by his Companion Mu'āz Ibn Jabal who wept at this speech

1539- Its circumstances have been detailed so: " The Prophet - *may the MOST HIGH LORD send Peace and Blessings on him-*

1540- ...Took one day Mu'āz on the pillion of his mount - *may GOD, Who preserves from disbelief and damnation, be Satisfied with him too -*

1541- [During the journey] the Chosen Prophet looked heavenwards and [after a while] uttered a praise to GOD, the BENEFACTOR

1542- After a moment of meditation, he called his Companion "O Mu'āz!"; this one answered: *"Here I am (Labayka), o Best of the creatures!"*

1543- Then [the Messenger] told him: *"I shall give thee a recommendation which will profit thee if thou put it into practice;*

1544- *But if thou disregard it, no excuse wilt thou have once before the LORD of the Heavens"*

1545- He gave him afterwards the advice above-mentioned; Mu'āz felt then a pang of anguish and of sorrow

1546- And his tears began to run down on his cheeks - *may GOD be pleased with him and with all that have followed him in Islam*

1547- We will now end this book in showing [at our turn] sense of ethics [vis-à-vis the MAJESTIC LORD]

1548- Because dealing with such things to which our LORD gives importance and which can lead to a happy end is part of the *adab* indeed

1549- After having finished in the finest way our undertaking here, now we do beseech the LORD to impart us too a happy end in the Hereafter

1550- ...By His Benevolence, His Nobleness, His Grace and His Infinite Kindness

1551- Here comes to an end "**WAYS UNTO HEAVEN**" by the Grace and the Help of our LORD, the BENEFACTOR

1552- Praise be to GOD Who has allowed us to complete this work after our undertaking to carry it out

1553- [Thanks must be rendered to Him] for these matchless verses whose beauty is beyond the Splendour of Hyacinth and Coral

1554- This work can indeed purify the heart [of any willing person] and can cure it of its vices

1555- It is endowed with so much wisdom about Sufism that it can assuredly suffice and replace all the books which have been previously written thereon

1556- ...By the Grace of [GOD], Who that holds whole Majesty and Honour - *may Thou grant me thereby all my needs!*

1557- May GOD rank this book among the *Ways* which lead truly *unto Heaven* all that have committed themselves into His Straight Path

1558-By His Infinite Grace, may He impart me as a Reward His Satisfaction, His Forgiveness and His Pardon

1559- May He provide us Delight, Lights into the grave, Security and Protection against any peril on the Day of Dreads

1560- I pray Him to bestow everlasting Peace and Blessings upon who that has rescued us from the Depths of Darkness

1561- ...The Prophet Muhammad, the Best of the Prophets, who that has bettered as well the lot of his neighbouring fellows as that of faraway creatures

1562- [May also such Peace and Blessings be lavished] upon his Honourable Kindred, his Valiant Companions - the True Worshippers - and all amongst the servants that are following in their footsteps

1563- This may be, as long as GOD will consent, by His Infinite Grace, to let the humble author of these verses[273] benefit from True Knowledge and as long as He will vouchsafe to grant him, thereby, a *Happy End*

O LORD!

Do grant Peace and Blessings

To our Master MUHAMMAD

---

[273] The Sheikh himself.

Lightning Source UK Ltd.
Milton Keynes UK
UKHW040630100521
383461UK00001B/71